EMBRACING
GOD

Also by Dwight H. Judy

Christian Meditation and Inner Healing

**Healing the Male Soul: Christianity
and the Mythic Journey**

EMBRACING GOD

Praying with Teresa of Avila

DWIGHT H. JUDY

ABINGDON PRESS
Nashville

EMBRACING GOD:
PRAYING WITH TERESA OF AVILA

Copyright © 1996 by Abingdon Press

This book is printed on recycled, acid-free paper.

Library of Congress Cataloging-in-Publication Data

Judy, Dwight H.
    Embracing God : praying with Teresa of Avila / Dwight H. Judy.
    p.   cm.
    Includes bibliographical references.
    ISBN 0-687-01000-4
    1. Teresa, of Avila, Saint, 1515-1582. 2. Spiritual life–Christianity.
3. Spiritual exercises .I. Title.
BX4700.T4J78 1996
248.3—dc20   96-21193
                                                          CIP

From *The Collected Works of St. Teresa of Avila, Volume One,* translated by Kieran Kavanaugh and Otilio Rodriguez, © 1976 by Washington Province of Discalced Carmelites, ICS Publications, 2131 Lincoln Rd. N.E., Washington D.C. 20002 USA.

From *The Collected Works of St. Teresa of Avila, Volume Two,* translated by Kieran Kavanaugh and Otilio Rodriguez, © 1980 by Washington Province of Discalced Carmelites, ICS Publications, 2131 Lincoln Rd. N.E., Washington D.C. 20002 USA.

From *The Collected Works of St. Teresa of Avila, Volume Three,* translated by Kieran Kavanaugh and Otilio Rodriguez, © 1985 by Washington Province of Discalced Carmelites, ICS Publications, 2131 Lincoln Rd. N.E., Washington D.C. 20002 USA.

The poetry in *The Collected Works of St. Teresa of Avila, Volume Three,* was translated by Adrian J. Cooney, O.C.D.

Scripture quotations are from *The New English Bible,* © The Delegates of the Oxford University Press and The Syndics of the Cambridge University Press 1961, 1970. Reprinted by permission.

96 97 98 99 00 01 02 03 04 05—10 9 8 7 6 5 4 3 2 1

MANUFACTURED IN THE UNITED STATES OF AMERICA

For Ruth Hagemeyer Judy,
friend and wife,
companion with whom I discover
the Divine Embrace

CONTENTS

FOREWORD

Your work is to discover your work
and then with all your heart,
to give yourself to it.

—Buddha

 aint Teresa de Avila continues to be an example of true heroism and deep commitment to making life itself a daily spiritual practice. As a feminine model, Teresa demonstrates the five essential qualities ascribed to heroes and heroines over the ages, more fully amplified in Miriam Polster's book, *Eve's Daughters: The Forbidden Heroism of Women:*

1. A profound respect for human life;
2. A strong sense of personal choice and effectiveness;
3. An original perspective on the world, going beyond what other people thought possible;
4. A demonstration of great physical and mental courage;
5. A commitment to meaningful action and a significant contribution, whether measured by public or nonpublic impact.

Teresa's *profound respect for human life* was included in all her writings and teachings. She reformed the Carmelite order and encouraged her nuns and her ally, St. John of the Cross (a Carmelite monk), to explore the interior world, but to do so in the context of broader service to the exterior world. Her belief was that any contribution—coming from love—enables the human enterprise.

Teresa's theology of the cross and constant seeking of the alignment of human and divine will were *pivotal in all her choices*. She was convinced that anything was possible or would be effective if human will and divine will worked together. Using this principle, she established seventeen Carmelite houses across Spain, the last one in the Basque village of Burgos. She was a passionate advocate for young women and was committed to creating environments within her convents where women would be free to turn inward and serve in the most effective ways possible.

Teresa was a visionary renowned for her spiritual revelations and instinctual capacity for mapping and codifying internal experiences. Her *original perspective* was to fully trust her own intuitive guidance, even when it went against the norms or established forms. During the Spanish Inquisition, she successfully used the feminine survival skills of anticipation, evading, and disarming her questioners, to the degree that the majority of her writings were impounded, rather than burned. She was lauded for her communication gifts, and still is regarded in the Catholic tradition as one who made the practice of interior prayer and the states associated with it most comprehensive.

Heroic courage requires both *physical and mental stamina*. Teresa was consistently challenged physically. Her health was her nemesis, and yet her mental conviction and undaunting spiritual quest and faith would not allow poor health to deter her travels, teachings, or writings. She believed that Christ's love would give her the strength to accomplish what was necessary.

During Teresa's lifetime, women were not accorded authority, autonomy, or power to any degree. Her mental acuity, courage, wit, humility, and deep faith in the healthy integration of compassionate work and unconditional love gave her the physical power and authority to accomplish all that she did in her sixty-seven years. Teresa believed in meaningful action and functioned as a spiritual teacher during the last twenty years of her life. Her goal was to teach others how to reach and explore the *interior castle*. Her joy was to watch as others moved through the seven interior rooms and experienced the spiritual states reached through contemplative prayer.

Saint Teresa was renowned and respected for her contribution during her lifetime. She was gifted in her capacity to inspire her communities, yet remained inherently private. Teresa found her greatest solace in contemplative prayer and silence. She sought no fame or public attention. Her commitment was to *meaningful action*, service, and soul work. She lived by her conviction: "Nothing is impossible when our Lord wants it."

Like Hildegarde of Bingen, Saint Teresa and her heroism, vision, and impact are reemerging as a source of spiritual inspiration today. Her biographers and translators (Auclair; Bilinkoff) have helped to clarify her legacy; yet this excellent book, as Dwight Judy has written it, opens the door to a more complete understanding of the relevance of Teresa's most important writing, *Interior Castle*.

Dr. Judy's insight and brilliant discourse of each of Teresa's seven interior rooms reveals an invaluable spiritual guidebook that can help the spiritual seeker of any tradition to open to the mystery of Divine Love and the true heroic journey.

ANGELES ARRIEN, Ph. D.
Cultural Anthropologist
Sausalito, California

PREFACE

hy another book on Saint Teresa of Avila? Her works have been translated into many languages. Her spirituality is studied extensively by the Carmelite women and men devoted to the spirituality she has left behind. Scholars have commented extensively on her writings.

What I hope to accomplish in this book is not to reiterate that scholarship, but to draw forth from her writings the essential core of her meditative prayer practice for people engaged in demanding, active lives. I hope to offer a guidebook to prayer that will be useful to a wide audience, especially to church leaders and laypeople who are working in the world. While Teresa's audience in her time was to monastics, there is a great need in our time for people engaged in demanding lives of public service to discover the inner serenity pursued by monastics in earlier times. Do we not also yearn to dwell in abiding union with God, in our everyday demands for meaningful work and family life?

It is important to realize that Teresa constantly asked herself whether her service to God resided more faithfully in her prayer life or in her life of active administrative duties. In fact, it seems to me that this is the formative question for Teresa's great period of service, from age forty until her death at sixty-seven. In this respect, it is highly appropriate that one who finds his or her own spiritual formation through the continual asking of that same question should bring Teresa's writings forth into a spiritual framework for the questions of our times. It has been my own personal challenge to ask this question much of my life: Is

God served most fully for me through prayer and reflection, or through active service?

The answer Teresa found for herself was that God seemed never to cease asking her to continue her demanding administrative challenges. Simultaneously, her great interior mysticism emerged. She offers a spirituality of interior development fully grounded in the active life of the world. For her, both interior life and exterior life are authentic expressions of Christian calling. Whether we approach her as the mistress of prayer or as the mistress of public service, we will find rich resources for our own life questions.

Thus, I approach her writings with the intent of speaking to the deep hunger in our time for meaningful connection to God, both within the recesses of our souls and outwardly in the domain of our deeds of public service. I bring my own struggle with these questions to Teresa's writings, as well as my constant concern for the expression of God's will through action and surrender within my life. I hope that my background in transpersonal psychology and liberal Protestant theology will offer some new insights into her works. Through the eyes of a Protestant minister, the eyes of a man, the eyes of a transpersonal psychologist, I will address the writings of this great Catholic woman and look for her essential prayer practice, especially in the *Interior Castle.*

Teresa wrote to renew the contemplative life of women in a time far different from our own. As a twentieth-century married American male and father, I could hardly stand farther outside that milieu. Furthermore, I stand outside both the Carmelite tradition and the Roman Catholic tradition. Nevertheless, the sixteenth-century woman who married God has found her way deeply into my own spiritual life.

I found myself quite captivated by Saint Teresa's writings more than fifteen years ago, in classes taught by Father Anthony Morello. Father Morello is a Carmelite who established a retreat center in Dallas, Texas—Mount Carmel, An Informal Center for Spiritual Education. At that time, in the late 1970s, I found substance in Saint Teresa's writings to assist me in a significant period of interior growth and development that was awakening in my life.

Subsequently, I have taught several classes and numerous workshops on the meditative prayer practice derived from Teresa's writings. I offer this interpretation of her meditative prayer practice and the spiritual growth that attends to the practitioners of her prayer, as a contribution to the current interest in spiritual development that abounds both within and beyond the church. In the last few years, during a time of great external demands from work and family, I have found Teresa, the administrator, serving as a model for me, holding forth the possibility of a deepening interior life sustained side by side with a demanding public life.

This book should be read with an attentive inward ear. Teresa is to be not only read but also heeded as a source of spiritual guidance. Her images often evoke profound response within us. In short, I hope that this small endeavor will make her simple and profound meditative prayer practice more accessible to many individuals who seek a renewed inner life.

I have often reflected on the image of Teresa renewing the contemplative life in her time as an appropriate image for the transpersonal movement in our time. Certainly the forms and the issues are different. Nevertheless, as we approach the twenty-first century, there is significant interest in the renewal of a meaningful contemplative life for our time. This reason alone is sufficient to stir our curiosity about a woman who went around Spain at the time of its greatest international power, calling individuals to poverty and inward surrender. She also stands as a model for those who would continue to make substantive contributions to their society in the second half of life. She is a woman of enormous courage—a powerful model for women and men of any age.

In writing this book, I have chosen to call her Teresa, rather than Saint Teresa, to bring her writings more directly into communication with our thoughts and interior strivings. After all, when she was writing this material, she was not canonized, but a fiery and often bewildered spiritual searcher and admin-

15

istrator. I think she would be happy to be called Teresa in a work dedicated to bringing her ideas to a wide audience at the end of the twentieth century.

I also have intentionally left out some portions of her writings. I have not dwelled on her use of language for the "world," such as a place with snakes and all kinds of vermin. It seems to me that now this language may be misleading. Teresa's intent was clearly not to negate our active life of service in the world. Her intent, when speaking negatively of the world, was to point out that being overly concerned with the material affairs of worldly life robs us of time and intention to pursue an inward understanding of deeper values and communion with God. However, I think her language in this case, while communicating effectively in her time, is not effective for our own time.

Also, I have not dwelled on her sometimes overly zealous reprimands of herself. Her writings often seem self-deprecating and overly focused on personal shame. Yet she also writes of the importance of having the right kind of humility. The wrong kind of humility is one in which we think so poorly of ourselves that we do not dare to approach God.

I have chosen to focus on her discussion of proper humility, rather than those parts of her writing in which she seems to indulge in the self-deprecating type of humility. Teresa's most mature writing focuses on the error we make by not daring to approach and appropriate God. She states that if we continually approach God and reflect upon ourselves in the light of God, then we will have a proper humility, as well as find the inward guidance for profound inner healing and active service. It is intriguing to note that Elizabeth Hamilton, one of Teresa's biographers, talks of this self-deprecating style in her writings. According to Hamilton, this style was utilized quite consciously by Teresa as a way of receiving more acceptance for her writings and that it was a useful convention for a woman writer of her time. If Teresa points out her own flaws, so to speak, then she is less apt to be reproached by critics of her writing and her inner experience. Hamilton shows that Teresa's personal letters are devoid of this kind of self-deprecation, but when she writes for public eyes, she effectively utilizes it (Hamilton, 1985, 26).

I will deal in a special way with still another very general area of Teresa's experience. Her prayer experience is extraordinary. She is a mistress of the soul comparable in style to some of the great Yogic masters. She was given to times of great absorption in prayer, when her attention to the outer world seemed to dissolve completely. In this respect, her experience is not an appropriate mirror for most of us. However, I think that to a lesser degree, these experiences are available to many people in our time. Thus I have taken the liberty to draw from her experience as an adept in prayer, but not to assume that it exactly mirrors the experience of spiritual seekers in our time.

Finally, a few words are appropriate regarding Teresa's writings. I do not find her easy to read. She is more imaginative than analytical. Thus, she often uses numerous terms for somewhat similar experiences. For example, *rapture, prayer of union,* and *spiritual delight*—all are used to describe similar experiences during deeply absorptive prayer. As I read and reread her writings, I continually discover subtle relationships among different terms. Since I have not read her in the original language, Spanish, it is important for me to acknowledge that this book is indebted to the excellent translation of Kieran Kavanaugh and Otilio Rodriguez. Some of the interpretations of her message are necessarily influenced by their terms. Teresa's language for God is predominantly masculine, although she uses feminine imagery in some of her writings. I have not changed any of these language forms, but have tried to be true to her diversity of descriptions.

In a workshop in which I presented the meditative practice of Teresa of Avila, I was given what I took to be a high compliment. One of the participants said he felt that he had just heard the *Cliffs Notes* version of Teresa's writings—those little pamphlets that give synopses of countless books for college-exam crammers. Something like that is what I hope I've accomplished here. I hope that I have said just enough to give a meaningful synopsis of her style of meditative prayer and spiritual growth.

If successful, this work also will provide guidance to those interested in reading her works directly.

This book has been prepared for use by individuals and by groups. At the end of each chapter, exercises for personal reflection and prayer are given, based on the content of the chapter. These exercises are beneficial for personal self-understanding, and they also can be utilized for group discussion. The first group of exercises in chapter 1 includes some guidelines for group use of this material.

During the time of writing this book, my own life has taken an unexpected turn toward a new mode of service. This change takes me from exploring the new spiritual quest as a faculty member at the Institute of Transpersonal Psychology to becoming Director of Oakwood Spiritual Life Center in Syracuse, Indiana. In this new arena, many opportunities are given for people to explore their callings from God for interior awareness and discernment of public service. In accepting this new challenge, I have been grateful for the wise counsel of Teresa's example in interior and exterior matters.

My fondest hope is that I have made some contribution in bringing forth for our time Teresa's message of divine love and her form of meditative silence. May she inspire us to the appropriate renewal of contemplative life and active service for the changes our world is undergoing as we end this millennium and begin the next.

Oakwood Spiritual Life Center
Syracuse, Indiana

CHAPTER ONE
Teresa of Avila
A Woman for Our Times

In Your hand
I place my heart,
Body, life and soul,
Deep feelings and affections mine,
Spouse—Redeemer sweet,
Myself offered now to you,
What do You want of me?

Give me death, give me life,
Health or sickness,
Honor or shame,
War or swelling peace,
Weakness or full strength,
Yes, to these I say,
What do You want of me?

From "In the Hands of God" (Vol. 3, 377-78),
The Collected Works of St. Teresa of Avila

his book is an invitation to friendship. Over the years that I have studied Teresa, I have come to call her "friend." In a way that transcends time, distance, and culture, I have found Teresa to be a confidant and sojourner for my own spiritual struggles. While no friend can

19

be expected to be a confidant in all matters of one's own spiritual journey, I have found Teresa to be extraordinarily helpful in the fundamental questions of faith, prayer, and service. She has served as both model and guide for balance in my own life, between the tasks of external service and the discovery of God in interior reflection. She has been my most astute guide to understanding the interior ways of perceiving God through prayer. She also has served as one of the most significant models in my life for continuing to persevere in tasks of service when difficulties arise. Her own tenacity in founding her houses of prayer across Spain is a model of perseverance in God's service for all ages. For such companionship, I am extremely grateful.

It is perhaps no surprise that *friend* would become the term with which I now approach Teresa, for *friend* is the category of relationship that underlies Teresa's own lifelong companionship with God. She embraced God as God embraced her. For her relationship with God, she freely used many different terms. Underlying each of these relationships is a companionship of intimacy and discovery: *discovery of herself and of God.* What more can we wish of friendship?

As we begin our exploration of Teresa's images of prayer, we will look for this whisper of divine intimacy within ourselves. I always recall with appreciation my first reading of Teresa's *Interior Castle*. From the beginning, as I read her words, God whispered within my heart, summoning me to a deeper friendship and companionship. As I studied Teresa, I found new experiences of God presenting themselves to me. When I first read *Interior Castle* so many years ago, I found myself swept up into many of the experiences of deep prayer that she described. When she spoke of God's presence, I too felt God present. She gave me a language of interior imagination and experiences of the heart, so that I could listen more clearly for God's guidance within my life. Through her writings, I understood God's presence more distinctly.

As we lay the foundation for this mutual discovery of intimacy with self and God, we will direct our gaze toward Teresa's own life and times. In this chapter we will glance backward, and then look at the challenges of our own present century. Teresa was a very astute political figure of her times. She had no problem with writing to the king of Spain regarding matters of concern to the women in her convents. She understood herself extraordinarily well as a person within a particular historical milieu. To fully appreciate the power of her spiritual direction for our own lives, we also must relate our discoveries in prayer to the challenges of our times.

In our time, many spiritually earnest people avoid contemplative skills or disciplines in prayer, thinking that a monastic or interior impulse is a withdrawal from social responsibility. The embrace of God for Teresa, however, meant an embrace that reached through the political struggles of her times and brought about very particular tasks. Is God also so intimate with us? Have we allowed God such direction over our actions? Teresa invites us to do so. Her experience of union with God is a union of the human will and the divine will for transformative action within human society. Surely, we each long for such certainty. We will find within Teresa's writings the emergence of a powerful personal authority rooted in the conviction of God's intimate presence and personal guidance. Let us begin our discoveries under Teresa's guidance, by exploring the milieu of her times.

SIXTEENTH-CENTURY SPAIN AND TWENTY-FIRST-CENTURY CHALLENGES

Born in imperial Spain in 1515, Teresa of Avila lived at a time that bears striking resemblance to our own. No less than the twentieth century, the sixteenth was a watershed in human consciousness. Less than a generation before her birth, Columbus had sailed for the Indies and discovered the West Indies, a new world for the Europeans. During Teresa's lifetime, Spain was growing in wealth, international influence, and domination. Global trade routes became abundant and well-established, swelling Spain's national treasury with gold and silver, giving Spain an imperial ambition for global domination and establishing her authority in Europe. By the end of the sixteenth century, Spain was overextended and overspending to maintain its imperial ambitions. Nevertheless, it is hard to imagine a more vital time in Spanish history. This vitality extended to the whole European continent.

The Reformation and Counter-Reformation mirrored a revolution in Western thought that gave birth to a dominance of rational process in the seventeenth and eighteenth centuries. The struggle for the mind of the West, with a shift away from allegiance to church and a growing thirst for wealth and economic expansion fueled the industrial revolution of the eighteenth century. Many of the inner movements leading to this broad change of Western thinking can be seen operating in the sixteenth century. Sixteenth-century Spain, I think, must bear a striking resemblance to the twentieth century as a time of the absorption of a whole new mind-set by a culture at large.

This epoch witnessed a profound shift in internal and external allegiances, as the supremacy of the church of Rome was challenged and political alliances over the face of Europe and the world were redrawn. Through trade, the European viewpoint was exposed to those of China, Japan, India, the Middle East, and the pre-Columbian Americas. Throughout the sixteenth century, Spain reaped wealth and prestige from its conquests.

If the fundamental allegiances of the European heart were being challenged during this century by an expansionist political and economic environment, the church of Rome reacted with vicious repression. The Inquisition in its various forms took root especially forcefully in Spain, under Jesuit influence. The links of economic secular power and religious authority found mutual strength as Spain sought not only to rule the world but to do so in cooperation with the church of Rome. Teresa, herself, prayed for the demise of the Reformers and hoped for the restoration of full Christian allegiance to Rome. In such an era of rising economic expectations and increasing wealth and influence for Spain, it is truly remarkable that Spain gave birth to three of the greatest mystic souls of Christianity—Ignatius of Loyola (1491–1556), Teresa of Avila (1515–1582), and John of the Cross (1542–1591). But perhaps it is not so remarkable. Perhaps God seeks to awaken new understandings of the depths of interior human experience during such times of great expansion of the human imagination as manifested in economic expansion and redrawing of maps of global influence.

I have spoken of Teresa as a woman for our times, because I do think there is a great parallel between the developments of the twentieth century and those of sixteenth-century Spain. We have seen, in fact, during the twentieth century, the demise of imperial methodology for global rule that was set in motion in the sixteenth. Whether a polyphonic empire such as the British Empire, with its attempt to rule in concert with vastly diverse cultures, or the monolithic empire of the communist U.S.S.R., with its dedication to central control, the great centralizing empires have fallen in this century. We have now seen ourselves from space. The human community is struggling toward new structures for economic and political cooperation among its vastly diverse peoples, as the revolution in communication technology makes us one world. We face nuclear and ecological dangers. This, no less than the sixteenth century, is a time of restructuring the human mind to face new challenges. At such a time, it is particularly useful for us to revisit the mind of one of the great soul-seekers of the West. In our times of challenge and promise, we need a renewed spiritual center within ourselves. In Teresa, we will find a guide toward this creative center.

In our time, as in Teresa's, there is great interest in mapping the interior space of human consciousness in a new way. Times of great social change and dislocation require a new discovery of the deepest human capacity for self-awareness and creative response. Thus it is perhaps not so remarkable that the geopolitical sixteenth-century upheavals would have been accompanied by visionaries of the human soul. In our time we find a great burst of energy and attention to this inner landscape of the human being in the fields of body/mind awareness, health,

23

Jungian psychology, the spirituality of addictions, as well as in a recovery of the essential mystical teachings of all the world's religions. For the past twenty-five years, transpersonal psychology has sought to create a unified arena of study and practice of the inner capacities of the human being for states of transcendent awareness, inner healing, and creativity. Our own century, with its vast redrawing of the geopolitical landscape, also has produced a vast remapping of the landscape of the human soul. Our time, no less than Teresa's, has called forth new attention to interior awareness.

Why might these two forces—the reshaping of external political and economic life and the renewal of interior mysticism—be companions? I think the answer is actually very simple and fundamental, and I find myself much influenced by Teresa in offering this answer: Fundamentally, each human being wishes for life to mean something beyond simple existence. In times of great exterior expansion, when the world order changes dramatically, we find it natural and necessary to look afresh into the human psyche to discern the deepest core within ourselves, where personal meaning and life direction are charted. When our worldview is radically expanded and altered, we need to find our internal compass afresh.

For Teresa, the guiding principle for this interior quest was to seek an alignment of the individual human will with the divine will. In our time, regardless of the language we use to speak of this principle, I believe that for most earnest people, each of us is seeking fundamentally the same thing Teresa sought. Today, many of us speak of God's will for our lives. Many others do not use that language, because "God's will" seems external to us, something to which we must conform. For Teresa, God's will was actually the deepest interior core of each human being. The search for "God's will" does not take me further away from myself, but further into relationship with myself. In Teresa's understanding, this search takes each of us through multiple interior realms, toward the greatest discovery of all. The core of my humanity is the divine core within me, seeking to give direction, meaning, and purpose to my life.

You may phrase this quest for God's will differently. You may ask: What is the purpose of my life? What should I do with my life during this phase? Should I go into or leave this relationship? Should I take this job or look for another? Is it time to retire, and if so, where will I live? Fundamental, I think, to all these types of deep life questions is another way of asking them: What is the will of God today for me in this matter? That is what Teresa would have asked.

In our time, Matthew Fox has spoken eloquently of the need to position our own acts of creativity within what he calls the *Via Transformativa*. He says that we are never really satisfied with our decisions, we never adequately answer the question of personal meaning, until we have understood the works of our life as a contribution to the transformation of the world (Fox, 1983). Teresa, I believe, would heartily agree. The deepest union between the individual and God is a union of will. For Teresa, spiritual maturity means that we will act day to day in concert with the great unfolding movement of God within our world. The quest for meaningful action, prompted by the divine will, was for Teresa the saving quest of human life.

TERESA'S ILLNESS AND CONVERSION

For the first half of her life, Teresa seemed destined to no particular greatness or notoriety. Between the ages of twenty and almost forty, she sought to live the life of a faithful nun of her day. It should be noted that while the Rule for the daily office was followed, monastic life in her time was influenced by other conventions. Either marriage or the convent were considered appropriate living arrangements for women of wealth and nobility. Often, women in the convent brought household servants with them and lived quite comfortably. Teresa, herself, fit this model to a great degree. She was given to times of gregariousness and gossip with her friends. In fact, as she later analyzed this period, she felt that far too often she had chosen to spend time in frivolous behavior, rather than in the exercise of her spiritual life. Later, she was to promote serious reorganization of monastic life.

When Teresa first entered the monastery, she was struck with a mysterious illness. The treatments of her day, such as bloodletting, seem to have debilitated her system so badly that she almost died. She writes that she was diagnosed with tuberculosis. In fact, in her autobiography, *Life,* she writes that she was so ill that she was presumed to be dead for four days. When she began to come out of that severe state, the wax of funeral candles had blown onto her eyelids (Kavanaugh and Rodriguez, 1976, 49-50). Fortunately, she survived this time of great distress and was gradually nursed back to health after several months in her father's house. From time to time in the next twenty years of her life, these mysterious illnesses returned.

It was not until she was thirty-nine that she spoke of her own true conversion—almost twenty years of monastic life before her interior conviction of God took root. She speaks of those years as being quite turbulent. Her mysterious illness returned from time to time, and she would return to her father's house to regain her health. She felt drawn to times of deep interior prayer, but was frequently advised against engaging in such prayer. In fact, even in her early twenties, she experienced the deep absorption in prayer that she called the prayer of union (ibid., 43).

However, she found very little support for such mystical tendencies and seems therefore to have experienced a great deal of confusion regarding her spiritual life. Later, she was to write that she felt that her spiritual growth was delayed because of poor spiritual direction. One of the intriguing aspects of her later life was that she learned to deal successfully with her illnesses and her interior life. I think that it is not inaccurate to say that her conversion was the beginning of her pathway toward successful management of both her illness and her mysticism. She writes that it was only after she stopped giving so much attention to her physical illnesses that she really began to improve. It was when she began to heed the call to service from deep within herself that she received fresh energy for life.

As long as she focused on her illness, she found herself further debilitated.

That illness may have been rooted in a psychological crisis, possibly resulting from a thwarting of her natural interest in a young man, which did not lead to a successful courtship and marriage. From the perspective of a Freudian interpretation, her illness took on the guise of a psychosexual hysterical conversion reaction, leading to debilitating paralysis and other ailments. In certain periods she writes of vomiting daily and of her own inducing of the vomiting (ibid., 60). Was this mysterious illness a severe form of bulimia, which then led to depletion of her immune system?

Perhaps all this psychological retrospection is completely false or speculative. She herself attributed the cause to poor food in the monastery, leading to a physical depletion! Perhaps her illnesses in later life were simply rooted in the severity of her early illness. We simply do not know, and we should acknowledge the inadequacy of any attempt to explain the nature of this illness.

But we do know from her own descriptions that she felt quite disconsolate over this recurring illness during her early adulthood, and it was when she truly felt God alive within her own being that she began her remarkable period of activity and influence in the world. It is when she made the link between her personal will and the divine will within herself that she began her own healing journey. This remarkable healing led to a life of robust activity after the age of forty.

Perhaps the very mysterious quality of her illness makes her appeal even greater for our time. All of us are wounded! Whether our wounds are manifested physically through recurrent illness or psychologically through patterns of personal despair or fragmentation, Teresa's healing may offer a pattern for our own needed healings. Teresa's healing springs from a spiritual source. It is fundamentally a change of perception that changes Teresa's life patterns. This change begins with a conviction that God dwells in her own being and seeks to give direction to her life. She was never without some physical

27

distress. However, she became a woman of enormous creativity when she learned to discern the wisdom of the interior God and to pay less attention to her infirmities.

Teresa offers each of us hope that in a time when great demands are placed upon us, springing from the external world and from internal stresses, and when even social and family systems of support are weakening, there is a source of interior wisdom and guidance that can inform us. Teresa calls this source of interior wisdom and guidance God, and finds that learning to discern God's claim upon us leads us toward deeds of meaningful service for the transformation of the world.

TERESA'S SPIRITUALITY OF THE CROSS AND DISCOVERY OF PERSONAL AUTHORITY

Teresa's mysticism is not a mysticism of particular interior states of consciousness. She is not aiming toward a union with God that leads to a certain type of bliss. Instead, she speaks of the primacy of the cross in her personal theology. She states that the awareness of God is not given merely to infuse us with good feelings, although frequently such good feelings do come. She says that we must pursue a more challenging spirituality than one of mere spiritual delight. Instead, we must choose the way of the cross.

This spirituality of the cross healed Teresa! For her, this spirituality and a spirituality focused on discerning God's will are one and the same. At stake here is an immensely challenging and empowering concept. God calls us to tasks beyond those we think we can perform, tasks leading to a renewal of society in love, tasks leading to serving others in pain or crisis. And in listening for and responding to this seemingly superhuman challenge, we also find ourselves guided away from debilitating physical and psychological weaknesses. Teresa came fervently to believe that God was present with her, transforming her personality and challenging her to deeds beyond her own capacity to fulfill. Because she heeded that inward challenge, she

28

renewed the monastic life in her time, established Carmelite houses across Spain, and wrote her guidebooks on the interior life. All of this, we might say, sprang from her inner source of creative, divine inspiration. When she heeded that interior voice, rather than her physical distress, she was so sufficiently energized that she has left a great legacy.

Teresa is a model not only in self-healing, but also a model for all people in midlife. She did not begin the great labors for which we remember her until age forty-seven. At that time she began her writings and the renewal of Carmelite monasticism. For the next twenty years she labored with these two great tasks, giving us eloquent writings on the inner life and leaving a legacy of a renewed Rule for contemplative life in her administrative work. Often she found these tasks, whether of physically establishing her houses of prayer or of writing, to be challenging tasks. Often she would have preferred the life of interior prayer and cloistered silence. But for Teresa, the active dimensions of God's will manifesting through her required deeds of administrative service and writing, undertaken beyond her own level of personal desire. She demonstrates a profound renewal in midlife for all who would heed the lifelong challenge to grow in God.

Teresa brought together all her acquired life skills—interior and exterior—to the tasks of mature adulthood. She is a great model of authentic service rendered in maturity.

Teresa is also a model for women of any age. Her era was a time when women were not accorded authority, autonomy, or power to any degree. The translators of Teresa's works quote from a writing attributed to Francisco de Osuna, contemporary with Teresa, which illustrates the degree of repression toward women in sixteenth-century Spain.

> Since you see your wife going about visiting many churches, practicing many devotions, and pretending to be a saint, lock the door; and if that isn't sufficient, break her leg if she is young, for she can go to heaven lame from her own house without going around in search of these suspect forms of holiness. It is enough

29

for a woman to hear a sermon and then put it into practice. If she desires more, let a book be read to her while she spins, seated at her husband's side. (Kavanaugh and Rodriguez, 1980, 23)

Teresa persisted in a world defined by cruel, widespread disapproval, not only of initiative in women but in particular of women actively pursuing matters of the Spirit.

It was especially suspect for women to engage in meditative prayer forms, in which Teresa clearly excelled. Throughout her life, she sought clarity with her confessors on these matters. Often they suggested that she should not give such credence to her own interior life. However, Teresa finally obeyed her own interior urgings on these matters by cultivating and describing her deep interior experiences. Her health springs from this emergent autonomy as well as from the active life, inspired from her interior prayer.

In an intriguing way, I find Teresa a superb model for men in our time. As we approach the twenty-first century, the cultural norm regarding interior development for men and women is the reverse of the norm in Teresa's time. Now it is more acceptable for women than for men to engage in interior development. Teresa's capacity to stand against the conventions of her day, to allow time for the cultivation of a rich interior life as a woman, offers a profound model for both women and men. Now men, in particular, may draw strength from Teresa's risking to know herself, as she stood against the conventional wisdom of her day that restricted such activities for women. From her example, the pathways of silence, meditation, and prayer are given prominence. In our time, when these activities are less honored, we may draw strength from Teresa to pursue them.

Teresa also offers a compelling model for contemporary spiritual development. She was in many ways a twentieth-century woman. Her great task was one of learning to trust her own intuitive guidance, even when it meant going against established forms and norms. She is a predecessor of the twentieth-century quest for individual autonomy and individual personal authority. In this respect she has much to teach us about making the quest toward personal autonomy, while also holding oneself accountable to a higher authority. Along with her evolving sense of personal authority in trusting her inner divine guidance, she made an effort to maintain clear thinking and theological correctness. She often went to theologians for discernment of questions of theology that arose from her interior experience. On this point, she provides a corrective to the extremely individualistic approach of twentieth-century spiritual development. Teresa would not have wished her meditative prayer practice to be used apart from a theology of surrender to the higher authority of God, which for her was characterized as the way of the cross. Today, the need is for vital forms of personal spiritual practice, linked with fresh understandings of the religious traditions from which they have sprung.

Having said that cautionary word, however, it is fascinating to view the authority with which Teresa describes her own spiritual experiences. She allows her own psyche the freedom to express itself. It is an image from her own deep prayer that most directly informs her understanding of the nature of God and God's relationship to the individual.

This is the image of the crystal or diamond suffusing light from its center. We will explicate this image through our description of Teresa's methods of prayer. I wish to point out here that once she received this image from her own interior, she used it with great liberty. She lets it stand alongside historic images of faith, such as the Holy Trinity and Christ, as a means of teaching interior prayer. Today such prayer images continue to assert themselves with authority. Often in times of deep prayer, an individual will receive a kind of personal revelation in a symbolic form, which then remains with her or him for a long time as a sustaining prayer symbol. For example, for many years, the word "Thou" contained this type of power for me. After meditating on the psalms for several months, the simple term "Thou" came to represent my full relationship with God. Although I have not used this word as my formal meditation

31

for many years, it still stirs me deeply when I ponder the term. It clearly holds great symbolic power for me.

For Teresa, the image of the crystal or diamond, with light emanating from its center and resting in her heart, conveyed to her the message, "God is within you, aligning his loving will and yours." So, as we approach Teresa's meditative practice, we will do so with the same sense of personal authority that she gave herself. Our task will be not to squeeze our inner urges into her imagery, but to utilize her methods to open the door for our own imagery to emerge.

Because Teresa allowed the psyche's imagery to flow unobstructed, I speak of her as a twenty-first-century woman. In our time, with an awakened sense of personal psychological development, we also need the creative breakthroughs that come when we let the deep psyche speak to us on its own terms. From that deep core comes the raw material from which we discern our creative actions of service in the world.

Teresa has much to teach us regarding discernment—what she calls the discernment of God's will. When we open ourselves to the many creative images the psyche presents, we find an array of experiences that sometimes baffle and confuse us rather than inform us with clarity. Teresa anticipates this problem. She has much to say about clarifying which interior voices and visions are most trustworthy in guiding us toward the divine will for our lives.

Teresa also anticipates our time in her very thorough discussion of the variety of interior experiences that can come in deep prayer and meditation. We find, particularly in Mansions VI of her *Interior Castle*, a great resource for describing unusual spiritual experiences. Contemporary interest in the phenomena associated with spiritual emergence finds a welcome companion in Teresa's writings. The new field of spiritual emergence in our time is cataloging unusual experiences of the psyche, as well as energy experiences in the body that at times accompany profound experiences of meditation and spiritual development (Bragdon, 1990; Greenwell, 1990; Grof and Grof, 1989; Grof and Grof, 1990). Many of these experiences are described in the context of the history of Western mysticism in Evelyn Underhill's classic, *Mysticism,* written in 1911 (1961). I have found it extraordinarily therapeutic to recommend the reading of Mansions VI to people undergoing dramatic spiritual experiences. Our culture, by and large, is so out of touch with these experiences that the individual experiencing them is often at a loss for meaningful guidance in understanding the dislocation of personality that comes with a period of radical spiritual transformation.

Teresa's own discussion of these matters is very refreshing and, I think, important for our time. She never seeks any of these unusual experiences. She does encourage us to spend time with God in meditative prayer. Her theology of the cross and of seeking the alignment of the human and divine will are pivotal. She does not promote a spirituality of psychic experience. Instead, she encourages our spiritual experience to evidence itself in meaningful social action. Thus, it seems to me, her writing provides not only companionship to those engaged in significant intrapersonal discovery, but also challenges us to bring the awakened self into significant action to meet the social and political challenges of our time. We will thus approach Teresa's spirituality with a keen eye toward action as well as contemplation.

TERESA'S GUIDANCE FOR OUR TIMES

I have mentioned the correlation between Teresa and her times and our contemporary times, but I would like to say a bit more about the present need for Teresa's guidance. If historians paint an accurate picture, a century ago there was a sense of great optimism regarding the beginning of the twentieth century. The industrial revolution had done its work, and living standards were beginning to improve. We certainly needed the muckrakers in the United States and elsewhere in the early part of the twentieth century to bring more order and justice to the life of workers, and we got it. A utopian vision swept through

33

Russia in 1917, but then became the dark specter of communist totalitarianism. Optimism gave way to tragedy as the Great Depression spawned Nazism in Germany, Stalinism in Russia, and other totalitarian forms of rule. Hundreds of millions of people have been killed in this century, in the name of questionable ideals of racial and ethnic purity.

And where was God during this century of holocausts? The biblical scholars, theologians, and even psychologists were so busy attempting to prove the validity of their voice, according to empirical scientific methods, that they stopped speaking to the plight of the individual human soul, struggling against the massive onslaught of raw violence that has swept across the world. After the disillusionment of World War II, even theology questioned God's existence. On the one hand we are making great strides in our understanding of the universe and human motivations, of ecological needs and political cooperation. On the other hand, we perhaps begin to have some genuine humility, recognizing that the human enterprise may not succeed in going through the passage that marks its entry into the twenty-first century. We are perhaps humbler and wiser, as a species, as we make this transition than we were as we made the transition into the twentieth.

In the last decade, street violence has skyrocketed in the United States. And we find all over the world that the Third World and the First World are next door to each other. First World and Third World meet in South Africa, but not only there. In every urban community in the United States, great wealth and grinding poverty exist next door to each other. For example, in the San Francisco Bay area, the community of Atherton with its $2 million properties, and East Palo Alto with its streets wracked by drug-related killings, are separated by one mile. Western Germany and Eastern Germany, with their vastly different economic histories, now seek to become an integrated national state. And we wonder how to support the emerging and very weak democratic structures in the nations of the former Soviet Union. Everywhere, we see a world either ready to face its diversity with its divisions of wealth and poverty, or a world ready to dissolve into a time of great chaos. The choice truly lies with every one of us and every one of our communities.

It is not surprising that there is now an attempt to again discover God within the depths of the human spirit. We desperately need an expanded vision of ourselves. We need models for exploring the depths of human experience, and we need the challenge toward meaningful service. We can benefit greatly from the example of a woman who overcame debilitating illness. Our social structures seem to suffer baffling illnesses that mirror Teresa's illness in an intriguing way. Periodically, we seem to find our whole social systems so fragmented that we seem weak, as Teresa was. Alternately, we seem to receive great hope. Perhaps this is a time of a birthing process in society, in which new forms of social health are being created. Clearly, it is a time when many old forms are dying.

I think that each of us personally participates to a much greater extent than we realize in these massive global challenges. The global uncertainty, as well as the threat of robbery to our homes or threat of violence to our ordinary existence, lurks with us on a daily basis. How are we to live with a sense of personal energy and creativity?

It is now that humanity needs the wisdom of all the great wise voices of human history to offer guidance. Teresa is one of those voices from which we can learn a great deal. From her, we learn first of all to listen deeply within ourselves. The solutions to our present dilemmas must come from fresh forms of social life and fresh inspiration. How will we discern those new directions? They must come from within an inspired humanity. Second, Teresa encourages us to discover ourselves, but to do so in the context of the broader service to the world. This is an especially critical message today. For the past fifty years, humanity has been struggling with the knowledge of its inherent bestiality as well as its potential for nobility. We will not solve our problems only through self-knowledge. But we can never solve our problems by avoiding self-knowledge.

35

Teresa taught the need for self-knowledge as a training in humility. Self-knowledge, even enlightened humble self-knowledge, however, is not enough to inspire us for these times. We also desperately need, each in our own way, to find what Teresa found and named as God—not a nameless God in some distant realm, but the God she knew so intimately that she called this One a Guest in the house of her soul. Do we believe that the source of interior motivation, joy, and challenge within ourselves, those interior voices that give guidance and direction to each of our daily activities, might actually be springing from a benevolent, creative God, and that this God is at the heart of every living thing, even at the core of the universe itself? Teresa so believed and was so inspired. It is clear that more than ever in human history we will not believe blindly in such a proposition, but we need to find methods to satisfy our own unique search. And Teresa provides such methods in her forms of interior knowledge and meditative prayer.

In one sense, Teresa offers us a road map for self-discovery. And she provides illuminative methods. However, I think her greatest gift is that she offers us a courageous model to begin our own quest to know ourselves and to find our deepest callings to service. She stands on the sidelines of history, watching us and cheering us on to take our times seriously, to take our intuitions seriously, and to offer the precious moments of our lives as a gift for the renewal of society. We must remember her challenge of poverty in a time of Spain's great wealth. What is the correlate in our time to this call to poverty? Each of us must risk asking that question and embracing the poor ones who live next door in East Palo Alto and East Germany and South Africa. Perhaps even more than material poverty, our time calls for a spiritual poverty, a true willingness to admit our emptiness of adequate solutions, our true need for the creative movement of God to inspire our actions. From that place of profound emptiness, we may yet discover within ourselves a divine voice whispering out of the silence, giving meaningful direction to our lives. Teresa will help us to discern that divine voice.

As we examine her model of spiritual development and her style of silence, we will explore the relationship between her methods and our present life issues. Chapter 2 explores her psychology of spiritual development and draws heavily upon the seven Mansions she describes in the *Interior Castle*. Chapter 3 examines particular methods of meditative prayer found in Teresa's writings and offers specific guidance in meditative prayer. Chapter 4 describes unusual spiritual experiences catalogued in her writings, with a special focus on discernment of the divine will. In chapter 5, we will discuss Teresa's focus on surrender and action as a framework for our own spiritual growth.

During the sixteenth century, Spain grew from a modest medieval political state to a worldwide empire. Unprecedented wealth flowed through its borders from its American colonies. It engaged in wars with rival European powers and remade the map of Europe through alliances. A dynamic middle class emerged. In spite of plagues, the population grew and prospered. During this time of dramatic change, the Inquisition sought to control religious thought, even impounding Teresa's writings. Yet the woman who married God went on about her tasks of calling for renewed religious vocation and the cultivation of silence. It is noteworthy that she wrote her greatest masterpiece on spiritual life, *Interior Castle*, after all her other writings had been impounded by the Inquisition, because her confessor, Father Gratian, asked her to do so. She undertook this task reluctantly at the age of sixty-two. Teresa was a force vital enough in her time to be noticed!

Our time, no less dramatically, witnesses enormous geopolitical changes. Our challenge also is to learn again the ways of silence and interior conviction. May Teresa assist us not only to make houses of prayer of the kind she made, but to make each of our homes and each of our hearts a house of prayer. And may she inspire us to act on our convictions in reshaping and renewing the social fabric of our world.

37

Exercises for Reflection and Prayer

Teresa comments that the way to deepening our spiritual life is through the twin modes of self-reflection and prayer. At the end of each chapter of this book, exercises are offered. If you are working alone with these exercises, you will find ample opportunity for keeping notes in a journal. You may wish to share your reflections with a trusted friend from time to time.

If you are reading this material with a group, find time within your group meeting to discuss the content of the chapter, and then in small groups, share some of your personal reflections on the exercises. There is ample material both in the chapters and in the exercises for reflection over several weeks' time. You may wish to undertake this as a 5–6 week study, focusing on one chapter each week and dividing your time between discussion of the chapter and sharing personal reflections. Because of the amount of content available here, a preferable way to use the material may be as a 10–12 week study, devoting one week to discussing the chapter and the following week to sharing material from the exercises.

It is vitally important to establish a climate of prayer and support in sharing the information that these exercises invite. It is very important to respect each individual's privacy. Much of this material is very personal in nature. No one should be asked to disclose more than he or she feels is appropriate. You may find that to build trust, it is useful to keep the same small group with whom you consistently share from week to week. Alternately, if you have a large group and wish to facilitate a deeper sharing within the whole group, it may be advantageous to randomly change your groups on a weekly basis. The whole group should discuss the options and decide together. You may wish to open and close the sharing time with prayer.

1. Relating to God

Describe your relationship to God. What images or metaphors help you to describe that relationship? Look back ten years. How is your current relationship with God similar to or different from the way it was then? Write a letter to God, telling about your relationship and describing how you would like that relationship to develop now.

2. Relating to the World

What areas of need within the world are most pressing upon you now? What concerns do you regularly bring to prayer? In what ways do you see hope for creative renewal within human affairs?

3. Rule of Life

Develop a "Rule of Life" for the time of this study, or for the next 1 to 3 months. A Rule of Life is a tool for personal attention, basically defining how you would like to grow spiritually. It is often developed on an annual basis to help chart personal spiritual disciplines. Areas that can be included in the Rule are Worship Attendance, Study, Service, Personal Prayer and Reflection, Physical Exercise, Time with Family. You can use the Rule to work on specific relationship issues. You also can look at your work priorities. A Rule can assist in setting specific areas of personal emotional response, such as curbing anger. You can be very specific or more general. The following chart may be useful in developing your Rule of Life.

RULE OF LIFE

For the period of time from _____ until _____

In the area of worship, I will: _____

As a personal discipline for prayer and reflection, I intend to:

_____

_____

When I think of issues within the world, I am most concerned about: _____

    In response to this concern, I will pray for: _____

    _____

    In response to this concern, I will serve through: _____

    _____

    In response to this concern, I will donate money to: ____

    _____

In other areas of service and work, I will serve God through:_____

_____

In my life of study, I will: _____

In my family life, I would like to: _____ _____

_____

In order to care for my physical body, I will: _____

_____

A personal issue/attitude I will observe is: _____

_____

If you have filled out something for all of these, it's probably too much. Go back and pick two or three of the most critical areas and notice whether you feel a true commitment to those. Underscore or highlight them.

In order to pay attention to these areas of potential development, I will review these areas on a daily and/or weekly basis, making journal notes of my relationship to the issue.

_____   _____
       (signed)   (date)

CHAPTER TWO
Teresa's Psychology of Spiritual Development

If the love You have for me,
Is like the love I have for You,
My God, what detains me?
Oh, what is delaying You?
—Soul, what is it you desire of me?
—My God, nothing other than to see You.
—What is it that you fear more than self?
—What I fear most is the loss of You.

From "Loving Colloquy" (Vol. 3, 380),
The Collected Works of St. Teresa of Avila

THE UNION OF DIVINE AND HUMAN WILL

he simplest way I have found to understand the psychology of the spiritual development of Teresa is to speak of the human being as possessing a divided self. We begin our deeper spiritual development as adults, possessing what twentieth-century psychology calls an *ego*. Yet there is an inward division between my ego-level will and the deepest desire of my human heart, which is the divine will. In fact, one might well say that each of these selves is a fully developed personality. Teresa's spiritual practice begins by urging these personality forces to become acquainted. Finally, a full union of the human with the divine personality and will is manifested.

It is impossible to understand Teresa's meditative prayer methods or her psychology of spiritual development without beginning with her understanding that God is already fully present within the individual, in the innermost recesses of our motivations, seeking to express the divine will. It is necessary, she writes, to "truly understand that within us lies something incomparably more precious than what we see outside ourselves. Let's not imagine that we are hollow inside" (Kavanaugh and Rodriguez, 1980, 144). Her language graphically illustrates this point with the images of her time. Imagine that God is a "mighty King who has been gracious enough to become your Father; and that He is seated upon an extremely valuable throne, which is your heart" (ibid., 143-44).

Much more is at stake in Teresa's image of God enthroned upon the individual human heart than an anthropomorphic and naive image. She herself is quite clear about the limits of such imagery. She calls this image "trifling" (ibid., 144), knowing that it cannot begin to contain the fullness of God. Nevertheless, she works extensively with imagery in order to communicate her thoughts to her audience, predominantly uneducated women. She consciously used imagery to convey ideas, and she herself was given to very provocative imagery in her meditative prayer life.

At stake in this imagery is a profound understanding that God is already fully present within the human heart. We need search no further than within ourselves to find God. Teresa is fully aware of the awesomeness of her comments. In many places she calls God the Emperor of the universe to point to the greatness of God. Yet this divine power is fully present within every human being.

In her commentary on the statement of the Lord's Prayer, "Who art in heaven," in *The Way of Perfection*, she elaborates on this concept:

You already know that God is everywhere. It's obvious, then, that where the king is there is his court; in sum, wherever God is, there is heaven. Without a doubt you can believe that where His Majesty is present, all glory is present. Consider what St. Augustine says, that he sought Him in many places but found Him ultimately within himself. Do you not think it matters little for a soul with a wandering mind to understand this truth and see that there is no need to go to heaven in order to speak with one's Eternal Father or find delight in Him? Nor is there any need to shout. However softly we speak, He is near enough to hear us. Neither is there any need for wings to go to find Him. All one need do is go into solitude and look at Him within oneself, and not turn away from so good a Guest but with great humility speak to Him as to a father. (Kavanaugh and Rodriguez, 1980, 140-41)

Teresa had very strong words to say about a false kind of humility in which we refuse to entertain the notion that God is fully available to us in the inward recesses of our solitude.

Leave aside any of that faintheartedness that some persons have and think is humility. You see, humility doesn't consist in refusing a favor the King offers you but in accepting such a favor and understanding how bountifully it comes to you and being delighted with it. What a nice kind of humility! I have the Emperor of heaven and earth in my house (for He comes to it in order to favor me and be happy with me), and out of humility I do not want to answer Him or stay with Him or take what He gives me, but I leave Him alone. Or, while He is telling me and begging me to ask him for something, I do not do so but remain poor; and I even let Him go, for He sees that I never finish trying to make up my mind. Have nothing to do with this kind of humility, daughters. (Ibid., 141)

This is a very radical notion for Teresa's time and for our time. How seriously does each of us take this Gospel imperative: the "kingdom" or the "realm" of God is at hand? The realm of God is within you. Teresa took this imperative of Jesus at face

44

value. And therein lies the profound inner healing work that her meditative prayer effects.

One of the present-day commentators on Teresa, placing her life in a psychoanalytic context, has written:

> To a reader who may somewhat share Teresa's belief systems, her life appears to be a series of miracles. Approaching her writings from another belief system, she remains a remarkable and creative woman. If one is not inclined to say that Teresa found God is it not also wondrous to say that Teresa found herself? That she approached the center of her own being and permitted the expression of a more "whole" Teresa? That she came as close as was humanly possible to healing herself? Neurotic patterns, once established, are difficult to change and, yet, through intense work, she changed her own. She managed to combine in her later life-style and self-image both the active and passive Teresa. She developed both the "masculine" and "feminine" of herself to express a unified exciting person. She found her own way of allowing her unconscious to surface and serve her needs. Whether we attribute her final successes to divine grace or to courageous struggle, or to both, it still was a process which produced a person remarkably healthy in the two basic areas that Freud used to measure healthy integration: love and work. Within her culture, Teresa succeeded in her work and in her love. It was not an easy task. (Romano, 1981, 293)

While not positing the miraculous at the exclusion of the genius of her own methods and the arduousness of her practice, I find her fundamental theological understanding of God's presence to be the single most significant factor in her own healing. The power of this concept must not be diminished by the elaboration of her methods or by seeking to understand her early life, with its baffling illnesses, from a clinical perspective. Teresa healed herself because she took seriously the central claim of Christianity—that God is in the world, God is in the universe, God is in the center of each human heart.

This God in the human heart is not a detached principle of creation. There is no *deus ex machina* in Teresa's spirituality. This God is a fully accessible generative power, actively manifesting goodwill toward the individual human being. This God, the Emperor of the universe, deigns to dwell within each of us, to share our lives, our struggles, and our redemption.

> But what a marvelous thing, that He who would fill a thousand worlds and many more with His grandeur would enclose Himself in something so small! [And so He wanted to enclose Himself in the womb of His most Blessed Mother.] In fact, since he is Lord He is free to do what he wants, and since He loves us He adapts Himself to our size. (Kavanaugh and Rodriguez, 1980, 144)

The most important concept in Teresa's psychology of the human being is the concept of the divided self. There is within each of us a fully active divine will and a fully active individual human will. For her, the fundamental task of spiritual development is the alignment of these two forces of will. Her method of interior prayer is a practice of profound listening for the wisdom of the divine will and learning to surrender the human will. This surrender, however, does not involve a wimpish or limp surrender in which one capitulates one's humanity. Instead, there is a vigorous training of the human will, a strengthening that is necessary before one is able to meet the divine will directly. Her spirituality of union between the human will and the divine will is aptly described as marriage. This union is first of all a union of two equal partners, the human will and the divine will. Only after this union of equals is there a final merging of the human personality into the divine.

Teresa's spiritual psychology and practice function to integrate the human personality and human will, while she simultaneously turns our attention toward the divine personality and divine will within ourselves. Again using the royal metaphor appropriate for her time, she speaks of the human faculties, such as the intellect and the feelings, as guardians of the interior castle of the soul in which God dwells. However, she says, these human faculties do not realize that there is a king within, and so each vies for supremacy as they argue constantly with each other. Her meditative practice enables us simultaneously to make peace with the interior human faculties while we learn to listen for the divine presence and guidance within ourselves. This integrative process is itself facilitated by the practice she describes as the prayer of recollection.

We shall have much to say about this practice in the next chapter when we explore the specific meditative practice of Teresa. But it is helpful to note here the capacity of this practice itself to assist us in integrating the human personality. "The prayer is called 'recollection,' because the soul collects its faculties together and enters within itself to be with its God" (ibid., 141). Thus, from a purely psychological perspective, her practice offers us an opportunity to quiet the internal chatter and divisions of our minds. From the standpoint of training of the human will, it provides an exceptionally productive method of training ourselves to focus our attention. Finally, this integrative process reaches beyond the personality of the individual to embrace God, as we each focus our attention not only on unifying ourselves but on the dynamic presence of God manifesting itself in the silence of our heart's solitude.

Thus there are many reasons for Teresa's method of prayer to draw us into a clearer relationship with ourselves, healing the many psychological wounds we bear. Finally, Teresa's method of prayer heals the wounds of separation between ourselves as unique personalities and all the rest of creation, the human family, the exigencies of life, and the divine mind itself. The final stages of her meditative practice bring us fully into relationship with God.

This process of alignment of the human personality and will with the divine personality and will is, for most people, a lifelong quest. The process of spiritual development that Teresa describes is not one that works quickly or effortlessly. She would have little tolerance for the offer of instantaneous enlightenment that many spiritualities promise in our day. For this wisdom, we can thank her twenty years of struggle with her own deep interior wounds and her search for appropriate spiritual guidance. In the mature writing of the *Interior Castle*, however, she has given us an extraordinary piece of guidance in the process of spiritual development that we may expect with a deepening prayer life. Although Teresa sought to disguise her own experiences when she wrote of "this person I know," it is very clear from her writing which experiences were hers and which were not. Thus we have preeminently in this work a description of her own spiritual pilgrimage.

I have described the focus and destination of Teresa's spiritual pilgrimage as union with the divine personality and will that is inherent in the human heart. This union manifests in the most interior region of the person. She describes this final stage in Mansions VII of the *Interior Castle*. It is important to notice at the very beginning of our quest for Teresa's spirituality that the destination of this process is very simple. For Teresa, the purpose of the interior life is good works: "This is the reason for prayer, my daughters, the purpose of this spiritual marriage: the birth always of good works, good works" (Kavanaugh and Rodriguez, 1980, 446). What an astonishing outcome! The spiritual struggle is finally about our life in relationship to the world. For Teresa, there is a litmus test of our spiritual life: Are we increasing our capacity for compassionate action in the world? Our prayer life, if authentic, will move us toward bearing worthwhile fruit in the world. Many Christian writers and teachers through the ages have said the same thing. In fact, a text from the New Testament that might well have been used by Teresa to underscore this type of thinking is Jesus' remark that "whoever does the will of my heavenly Father is my brother, my sister, my mother" (Matt. 12:50).

It is remarkable that Teresa's use of this test of spirituality comes at the conclusion of one of the most artful texts in Western literature on the development of interior life. It is far too common in our day for the two worlds, the outward world of service and the inward world of self-knowledge, to be considered separate and competing worlds. Teresa has none of this false dichotomy. For Teresa, inward knowledge is necessary for true compassion, because self-knowledge brings true humility. Thus for Teresa, wherever we go in the vast interior regions of our soul, we always go through the house of self-knowledge. "Can there be an evil greater than that of being ill at ease in our

48

own house? What hope can we have of finding rest outside of ourselves if we cannot be at rest within" (Kavanaugh and Rodriguez, 1980, 302).

The process of spiritual growth for Teresa involves continually looking in both directions, toward greater self-knowledge and toward greater knowledge of God. Without our gaze upon God, we will find ourselves unable to be freed "from the mud of fears, faintheartedness, and cowardice" (ibid., 292). However, without the practice of self-knowledge, we are tempted to "fly off to other rooms" (ibid.). This flight is clearly a flight into fanciful spiritual experiences without grounding them back into the personality. Teresa sets the stage in Mansions I of the *Interior Castle* for a spirituality that simultaneously expands us toward God and brings every insight back home to our human personality. She says that this dual approach helps us learn true humility and also assists the intellect and the will to "become nobler and better prepared for every good" (ibid.). Thus her process of meditative prayer is a process of grounded self-examination, as well as a process of deeper knowledge and experience of God. The two centers within the divided self, the human personality and will and the divine personality and will, thus learn to commune with each other through the constant attention given to each.

This practice of dual attention is a very practical tool for everyone engaged in serious spiritual practice. There is a demoralizing effect of constant self-examination, constant scrutiny on our faults and personality defects. Teresa suggests that this type of self-examination must be balanced by the ennobling practice of loving God. If this love of God is directed inward, we also readily see how it becomes a builder of communication with the deepest sources of creativity and wisdom within ourselves. Conversely, unusual spiritual experiences *per se*, flights into various interior mystic realms in and of themselves, hold no fancy for Teresa. Are our spiritual experiences deepening our love of God, our growth in personal humility, and our capacity for good works? If they are not, we are not on the pathway of true spiritual development.

Teresa frequently used this principle in her spiritual direction for the women with whom she lived. Sometimes they would come with tales of long prayer times and exquisite inner experiences. She once asked such a person: "But can you still sweep the floor?" On other occasions, she took meditative prayer away from people if they were becoming too absorbed in their inner experiences. I have made similar recommendations from time to time. Often our inner world will give us very powerful information. It may be necessary to have some time apart from meditative prayer to think through or talk through these experiences with a trusted counselor. Sometimes when we are finding places of deep hurt within ourselves, the most beneficial thing we can do is engage in some act of simple kindness for another, rather than focusing all our attention on our own pain. The key for Teresa is always balance of outward and inward attention, as well as balance between solitude and community connections.

This starting point is extremely important, because Teresa's prayer method leads to periods of profound inward silence, opening us to deep interior mystic experience. She thus lays the groundwork for these experiences to deepen us into God and our true self, while keeping us fully alive to the concrete issues of our world and our time.

In setting the groundwork for this discussion of the process of spiritual growth elaborated by Teresa in the *Interior Castle,* it is useful to mention one more aspect of the final destination of this process. Teresa is a master of the use of imagery, and she uses this well to communicate her meanings. This image of God enthroned on the heart was already present in her earlier writing in *The Way of Perfection,* in which she described this interior palace:

> Well, let us imagine that within us is an extremely rich palace, built entirely of gold and precious stones; in sum, built for a lord such as this. Imagine too, as is indeed so, that you have a part to play in order for the palace to be so beautiful; for there is no edifice as beautiful as is a soul pure and full of virtues. The

greater the virtues the more resplendent the jewels. Imagine, also, that in this palace dwells this mighty King who has been gracious enough to become your Father; and that he is seated upon an extremely valuable throne, which is your heart. (Ibid., 144)

This image is given a luminous aspect in the *Interior Castle*. She speaks of this divine center as "the shining sun" (ibid., 289). Sometimes she describes this luminous center as shining through a crystal or a diamond, or as a radiant Christ figure. This luminosity will become important in her later descriptions of the higher stages of prayer. But it is also an important symbolic representation of the immanent God inherently present in the human heart. Her image of sin is based on this luminous presence within the silent recesses of the human being.

> It should be kept in mind here that the fount, the shining sun that is in the center of the soul, does not lose its beauty and splendor; it is always present in the soul, and nothing can take away its loveliness. But if a black cloth is placed over a crystal that is in the sun, obviously the sun's brilliance will have no effect on the crystal even though the sun is shining on it. . . . O Jesus, how sad a thing it is to see a soul separated from this light! (Ibid., 289)

The luminous God is always present! However, the crystal may be covered with a black cloth or covered with pitch, so that the light cannot get out to illumine all the rooms of the castle. Here is a profound understanding of God as immanent in the human soul. The task of personal purification and of awakening to this inner light is the task of spiritual growth. This is a very important aspect, I think, of the profound inner healing manifested in Teresa's own life. It is not that the divine must be "added" to the human being. The divine is always fully present in splendor; however, it may be hidden. Teresa's greatest inward suffering was to realize how very cut off so many people were from this experience. They live in sin, in ignorance of God's presence within them. Thus, the very act of turning toward and claiming this interior light brings healing and ennobles the human personality.

Her passage into the interior castle is a passage toward this luminous divine center. It begins from the outermost level and moves inward. Each level in this development is itself a complex adventure. Teresa was quite clear that although she was using what we would term a "stage" model of development, individual experience is a much more complex arrangement than moving simply from stage to stage. "Thus I say that you should think not in terms of just a few rooms but in terms of a million; for souls, all with good intentions, enter here in many ways" (ibid., 293). Her language also speaks to this theme. She uses the plural, Mansions, to describe each level, which is thus seen as complex, with many, many subtleties. Her view is as close as one can come, I think, to incorporating the sense of internal multiplicity that we each encounter in our own spiritual pilgrimage, while also pointing to the landmarks in the pathway of spiritual development.

I have said that for Teresa this pathway is a passage toward the divine luminous center. That is only part of the dynamic, for this pathway of spiritual development and psychological healing is also a reaching out of the light of God to penetrate into the totality of the human personality. Thus a true dialogue takes place in this process, and a true intermingling of the divine with the human creates the transformed human personality.

MANSIONS I

The starting point of this journey of transformation for Teresa is in Mansions I, where people are very much concerned with outward life and worldly affairs, "engulfed in their pleasures and vanities, with their honors and pretences" (ibid., 293). Sometimes people think deeper thoughts, but in Mansions I they usually are buffeted about by their desires and outward things. They are, in fact, very unaware of their motivations. The door to the interior castle is "prayer and reflection" (ibid., 286).

It is clear that people in Mansions I practice very little prayer or reflection. The task here for the soul is to learn "to enter itself" (ibid.). The great need within Mansions I is to begin to cultivate a disciplined life of prayer and reflection.

Teresa's primary method for this disciplined prayer and reflection is reflection upon both self and God. "Our intellects and wills, dealing in turn now with self now with God, become nobler and better prepared for every good" (ibid., 292). The spiritual training, thus from the beginning, engages both centers of personality—the human and the divine. In so doing, we find an ennobling of our intellect and a training of our will. In order to penetrate more deeply into this interior castle with its mysteries and splendors, Teresa advises us "to give up unnecessary things and business affairs. Each one should do this in conformity with his state in life" (ibid., 294). Teresa challenges us to discern those activities that are truly necessary and those that lead us toward vanity.

She advises us to examine our traps of "possessions, honor, or business affairs" (ibid.). It is intriguing that she speaks of our doing this in conformity with our state in life. All of us must make this examination and these choices for ourselves. In fact, she speaks especially to those women who have given up outward things and entered the convent. Even for these, the worldly matters persist in a "zeal for perfection" that creates disharmony in the community (ibid., 295). She cites, for example, women who are overly zealous in the practice of penance. This overindulgence in spiritual practice produces a fierce judgmentalism toward other women in the community. It is important to note that for Teresa, such behavior is equal, in its distractions from the deeper life, to business affairs.

Thus for Teresa the issue is not the specific type of worldly action that distracts us, but that which stands between us and "love of God and neighbor" (ibid., 295-96). We begin the interior journey with discernment of our daily life for its traps and limiting behaviors that distance us from love.

MANSIONS II

The task of Mansions II is perseverance. Teresa admonishes beginners of meditative prayer not to look for particular types of spiritual experiences, for consolations, or for spiritual delights. The common theme addressed from several different perspectives in Mansions II is that we engage in this prayer to begin the task of alignment of the human will with the divine will, not for particular ecstasies and spiritual rewards.

She calls upon the example of the passion of Christ to help us. Our task, in short, in Mansions II, is to begin the arduous process of transformation, simply because we are called to it.

Even so, moments of clarity and presence of God do arrive in Mansions II. In a profound way, because they are more frequent than in Mansions I, or because we become more adept at perceiving these moments of presence, Mansions II actually becomes more difficult than Mansions I. In other words, as we begin to taste moments of God's presence, we begin to long for more. These moments come primarily through external means: "through words spoken by other good people, or through sermons, or through what is read in good books, or through the many things that are heard by which God calls, or through illnesses and trials, or also through a truth that He teaches during the brief moments we spend in prayer" (ibid., 298).

These moments of insight and inspiration seem to be balanced by a cacophony of temptations. "O Jesus, what an uproar the devils instigate here" (ibid., 299)! Buddhist tradition speaks of the great threat of doubt in the early stages of meditation practice. Teresa, I think, is speaking here of the same negative force. In every conceivable way, temptations abound: others' opinions of our undertaking this deeper spirituality, concern over our health, questioning whether we should spend our time in prayer or pursue temporal pleasures. This is the place where we learn what Teresa calls perseverance. As we begin to seek the only peace and security that can be found—that which is located within our own souls—every lesser security seeks our attention to distract us from this task. This challenge of lesser desires manifests even in an excessive worry over the lives of others. And it manifests in wanting the pleasures of meditative peace to develop quickly. To all of this, Teresa boldly proclaims: "Embrace the cross your Spouse has carried and understand that this must be your task" (ibid., 301). Our task is not the simplistic task of quieting the mind or stilling our stress responses, or deepening our self-awareness to the point where we live life with more tranquillity. All these blessings and many more may come.

However, the heart of Teresa's call to prayer goes to a much more strenuous discipline. "The whole aim of any person who is beginning prayer . . . should be that he work and prepare himself with determination and every possible effort to bring his will into conformity with God's will" (ibid.). Everything else is secondary. This concept of the alignment of the human and divine will is the most important of Teresa's conceptualizations regarding our prayer. Without it, she would find deep prayer and meditation a series of disjointed exotic experiences. With it as the ballast for our spiritual development, meditative prayer becomes an essential discipline for our transformation.

It is especially important in our time to dwell on this point. In an age in which meditative spiritualities are often taught as an end in themselves, it is critically important that we understand that in all the historic spiritual traditions, prayer is only one discipline of spiritual life. For Teresa, the task of spiritual life is ultimately a task of active life in the world. It is a task of discernment of meaningful service. It is the task of aligning our own will with the supernatural will, the will of God that unites all creatures and the universe in love. Perhaps for this reason one of her favorite and most used metaphors for God is Emperor of heaven and earth. God is the supreme force. Our task is to become consciously a part of that force.

In her own culminating visionary experience of union with the Holy Trinity, some six years before the writing of the *Interior Castle*, she describes this experience in concepts that underscore the alignment of human and divine will for which she strove in her prayer.

May 29, 1571 . . .
And so it seemed that all three Persons were represented distinctly in my soul and that they spoke to me, telling me that from
this day I would see an improvement in myself in respect to three
things and that each one of these Persons would grant me a favor:
one, the favor of charity; another, the favor of being able to suffer
gladly; and the third, the favor of experiencing this charity with
an enkindling in the soul. (Kavanaugh and Rodriguez, 1976, 327)

For Teresa, it is abundantly clear that her spiritual awakening
is an awakening of charity, a capacity for suffering in the deeds
of charity, and an enkindling spiritual fire to sustain these
actions.

After one month's time, during which this visionary experience remained very present to Teresa, she reflected further on
the experience and understood God to be saying to her, "Don't
try to hold Me within yourself, but try to hold yourself within
Me" (ibid., 328). This experience of the three "Persons" was
being communicated "to all creation without fail, nor did they
fail to be with me" (June 30, 1571) (ibid.). In July 1571, as she
tested again within herself whether she should be founding
monasteries or instead be always at prayer, she received this
message: "While one is alive, progress doesn't come from trying
to enjoy Me more but by trying to do My will" (ibid.). Thus we
see that even in the depths of Teresa's own prayer, her spirituality is confirmed again and again as a spirituality of action
within the world.

Such life-altering experiences come from time to time along
the pathway of Christian spiritual life. They are those major
shifts in awareness, those moments that form our personal
spiritual autobiography. In fact, they change our relationship to
both God and self. One of my earliest such experiences came in
my late twenties or early thirties. The thought came to me while
on vacation at Lake Michigan, that even though I had espoused
belief in the resurrection, even though I had preached the
resurrection, fundamentally I lived deep within my heart as a
follower of Christ crucified, but not yet resurrected. My spiri-

tuality was formed in imitation of Christ, the suffering servant, crucified. That day, I could almost imagine a fence between the two ways of living. On one side was life in imitation of Christ, crucified. On the other side of the fence was life lived in the presence of the resurrected Christ. As I walked the beach that day, I decided deep within myself to "jump" over the fence, to live in the presence of the resurrected One. Many changes followed that decision. In fact, I could now say in retrospect that it was the decision of my spirit that led me to my own midlife awakening to prayer, meditation, and the processes of inner healing. It began a fifteen-year journey.

During those fifteen years, my psyche itself has changed, first bringing an awakening of interior imaginative forms through dreams and meditative prayer. When the symbolic realm of my own psyche had been awakened, then the inner Christ came alive and has now become my companion for exploring and releasing issues of struggle and pain. In those cases, Christ as the inner healer is present. But I also have come to trust this inner Christ as the source of guidance and wisdom for questions regarding life decisions and life direction. This is the crucified and resurrected Christ to me, a source immediately and very directly present for healing, wisdom, and guidance.

It is little wonder then that in the early stages of disciplined meditative prayer, every distraction should attempt to dispel us from so great a task. The ego rightly fears that much will change! Teresa suggests that the intellect can be an aid at this stage: "The intellect tells the soul of its certainty that outside this castle, neither security nor peace will be found" (Kavanaugh and Rodriguez, 1980, 299). Teresa also suggests that for sustaining conversation, we need to find others who have traversed the way of this interior castle. Consult, she says, "with persons of experience" (ibid., 303).

She offers much more advice for beginners in her *Life*. There she speaks of putting oneself in the presence of Christ during inner meditation (Kavanaugh and Rodriguez, 1976, 93). This interior Christ becomes for Teresa a guiding meditative force. And for her, the interior Christ is the same Christ as the crucified and resurrected Christ of Scripture. In fact, she found herself energized when she stopped paying morbid attention to her physical illnesses, but instead embraced the task of service to Christ. Her own healing, in large measure, seems to have come from a cognitive decision to embrace the life of active charity.

> Since I am so sickly, I have always been tied down without being worth anything until I determined to pay no attention to the body or to my health. Now what I do doesn't amount to much; but since God desired that I understand this trick of the devil, who put the thought in my head that I would lose my health, I said: What difference does it make if I die; or at the thought of rest, I answered: I no longer need rest but the cross; and so with other thoughts. I have seen clearly that on very many occasions, even though I am in fact very sickly, that it was a temptation from the devil or from my own laziness—for afterward when I wasn't so cared for and pampered, I had much better health. (Ibid., 91)

So we begin to see both the seed of inner healing and the reward. They are one and the same—an increasing nonattachment to the minor though often commanding voices within ourselves, and an increasing discernment of the One true voice, the voice of divine compassion that draws us forth to active service in the world.

At the beginning stages much effort is required. In *Life*, Teresa speaks of this task as being like getting water from a well with a bucket. A great deal of effort is required on our part. As we will see in our discussion of Mansions III, this effort is essential because it is a cultivation of the will toward the service to which we are called, as well as a cultivation of the capacity of the will to focus our attention within the inward cacophany. Through the rigors of these trials, our spiritual task is to become "servants of love" (ibid., 78).

MANSIONS III

Mansions III is the preeminent level for the cultivation of the human will. Those who have entered this arena of spiritual development have found a certain "security of conscience" (Kavanaugh and Rodriguez, 1980, 304). As soon as Teresa writes the word *security,* she corrects herself to say that nothing is fully secure in spiritual life. Our only security is to keep ourselves on this path. However, her choice of terms is useful. For in Mansions III, people have found an equilibrium of spiritual practice that is both a blessing and a trap. Their lives do indeed have the connotations of security. And therein lie both the rewards and the problems of this stage of development.

These people practice well the Christian virtues of prayer and service. Their lives are "upright" and "well-ordered" (ibid., 309). Although a few of Teresa's terms are somewhat dated for our time, I think it is best to let her own words speak regarding these persons:

> I believe that through the goodness of God there are many of these souls in the world. They long not to offend His Majesty, even guarding themselves against venial sins; they are fond of doing penance and setting aside periods for recollection; they spend their time well, practicing works of charity toward their neighbors; and are very balanced in their use of speech and dress and in the governing of their households—those who have them. Certainly, this is a state to be desired. And, in my opinion, there is no reason why entrance even into the final dwelling place should be denied these souls, nor will the Lord deny them this entrance if they desire it; for such a desire is an excellent way to prepare oneself so that every favor may be granted. (Ibid., 306)

So what is the problem? The problem is that at this point, you have not yet surrendered fully to God. Your own will and effort have brought you here. You are like John Wesley's "almost Christian," who does all the right things a Christian does, but has not been awakened to Christ as an interior source of life. This description could well have been made of Wesley before

59

his Aldersgate experience, in which the inward conviction of Christ's forgiving love came alive for him.

Having reached a certain stability of practice, the great danger is spiritual pride and forgetting what Teresa calls the fear of God. Now this fear of God is equivalent, I believe, to awe, or approaching God in mystery. Because these people have made such progress and so much has depended upon their own willpower, they have not yet surrendered into the divine mystery.

Teresa cites the rich young man who came to Jesus, saying he had fulfilled all the religious laws, yet clearly did not find that enough to feel spiritually awakened. Jesus commanded a total surrender: He must sell all that he has and give it to the poor, and then he can come and follow Jesus. And because he was very rich, he went away sadly. Well, contrast such a response with Francis of Assisi, who did give up all his wealth and found eternal joy.

The great challenge of Mansions III is to heed the call to a deeper spirituality. Consider your response to life's trials. Teresa is baffled by people who have been in spiritual practice for many years, yet when life confronts them with challenges and struggles, they often respond with feelings of victimization. Suppose you lose some of your wealth. Or suppose your honor is questioned. How will you react? Teresa suggests that you would, of course, react with your feelings disturbed. And she is quite distressed and even, she says, afraid of the reaction of some of the virtuous people in Mansions III, who then long afterward castigate themselves for their initial feelings toward these trials. Or suppose one really has enough wealth for comfort and yet continues to worry over the accumulation of more. Or suppose one is overly concerned with worldly recognition and honor. All these things are traps of the passions. "[Y]ou can very well test and know whether or not you are the rulers of your passions" (ibid., 311).

It is intriguing that Teresa dwells on the personal feeling state of people in Mansions III. There is an absorption, you see, with oneself in this place, an overindulgence in one's feelings. At the same time, there is a failure to understand and heed the possibility of a deeper call to surrender to the divine will that will move us beyond such immediate concern with our feeling states. Our task, she writes, is to find "freedom of spirit" (ibid., 310). One might well say that in Mansions III, the human personality and will are still very much in control. They are in control in a reactive way in the personal absorption with feelings. And reason seeks to control our choices. "Love has not yet reached the point of overwhelming reason" (ibid., 312).

Many other Christian writers have sought to make this point. John Wesley wrote of the "almost Christian," who outwardly did all the right things but was not yet stirred at heart (Sugden, 1921, 1968).

Søren Kierkegaard (1958) wrote similarly of the great difficulty of Christians in his time moving beyond the veneer of an active life of virtue to discern the deeper stirrings of the spirit. Teresa faced the same problem in the convent:

> And believe me the whole affair doesn't lie in whether or not we wear the religious habit but in striving to practice the virtues, in surrendering our will to God in everything, in bringing our life into accordance with what His Majesty ordains for it, and in desiring that His will not ours be done. (Ibid., 311)

In short, people in Mansions III become "so circumspect, everything offends us because we fear everything; so we don't dare go further" (ibid., 312). This is a very significant stage, because much has been accomplished. Yet there is a need to understand and proceed from a deeper humility, a humility that now possesses a kind of holy abandonment of ourselves into the possibilities of a divine life. Teresa, in fact, invites us to let love overwhelm reason in our actions and in our interior world.

To aid us in this task, she suggests seeking sound advice from people who are "free from illusion about the things of the world" (ibid., 314). From these spiritually mature individuals, we can learn the freedom of spirit that comes from a deep commitment to live under the will of God rather than under our own will. "And it helps also because when we see some things done by others that seem so impossible for us and the ease with which they are done, we become very encouraged. And it seems that through the flight of these others we also will make bold to fly" (ibid., 312).

Teresa begins Mansions III with a description of a life too guarded and circumspect. She ends with a challenge to "abandon ourselves" into God. "With humility present, this stage is a most excellent one. If humility is lacking, we will remain here our whole life—and with a thousand afflictions and miseries. For since we will not have abandoned ourselves, this state will be very laborious and burdensome" (ibid., 313). This challenge of abandoning ourselves into the will of God finds a parallel in *The Way of Perfection*. There she challenges the women of her time to receive the divine Guest within the house of their souls and to commune with Him:

> I consider it impossible for us to pay so much attention to worldly things if we take the care to remember we have a Guest such as this within us, for we then see how lowly these things are next to what we possess within ourselves (Ibid., 144). For, in my opinion, if I had understood as I do now that in this little palace of my soul dwelt so great a King, I would not have left Him alone so often." (Ibid., 144)

Teresa's methods of prayer encourage freedom: "[S]peak with Him as with a father, or a brother, or a lord, or as with a spouse; sometimes in one way, at other times in another; He will teach you what you must do in order to please Him" (ibid., 141). Teresa's prayer is a practice in freedom of spirit and a focus of our faculties toward God, so that we may more and more regularly commune deeply with God and begin to understand the divine will more clearly. But Teresa's God also practices respect toward us. "And since He doesn't force our will, He takes what we give Him; but He doesn't give Himself completely until we give ourselves completely" (ibid., 145). The task of Mansions III, after we have learned self-discipline, is to decide to give ourselves completely to God.

Teresa speaks of the encouragement we can receive at this stage from reading spiritual texts about other people's experiences of consolations in prayer, or of deep tranquillity or profound experiences of God's presence. These can encourage us to move on more deeply—yet we must not fret if they are not present with us in Mansions III. For Teresa, these experiences come from the divine source. They cannot be manufactured by us. Our part is to persevere in prayer and an attitude of surrender. We must not wish for more than we receive of these types of experiences, yet the paradox is that their existence can provide encouragement for us to persevere in prayer. Even in light of this possibility, Teresa draws us back to the fundamental quest for the divine will to operate throughout our life: "We are fonder of consolations than we are of the cross" (ibid., 309). She challenges us to find our love of the cross equal to the inward tranquillity of consolation in prayer. By heeding this challenge, we will grow in spiritual maturity: "Enter, enter, my daughters, into the interior rooms; pass on from your little works" (ibid., 307).

MANSIONS IV

As Teresa guides us into Mansions IV, she writes some of her most sublime descriptions of deep prayer. She explains the subtle experiences of deep silence. She uses two key terms to describe these experiences: consolations and spiritual delights. The Spanish words are important in this case. *Contentos* is translated as *consolations*. These are experiences of "joy, peace, satisfaction . . . similar to those derived from everyday events" (ibid., 487). *Gustos* are experiences, described as *spiritual delights* of "infused, 'supernatural,' or mystical prayer" (ibid.). Mansions IV describes the intermingling of these two types of experience.

If you will recall the concept of the divided self with which we began this chapter, you will understand the distinction Teresa is making here. In Mansions IV, God begins to commune directly with us. The divine center awakens. In those moments, when "His Majesty desires the intellect to stop, He occupies it in another way and gives it a light so far above what we can attain that it remains absorbed" (ibid., 336).

Teresa also speaks of physical experiences that at times accompany *gustos*. In addition, she names a particular type of prayer and a type of method that we should employ when God begins dwelling with us in this infused way—the prayer of quiet. This small chapter is thus an extremely important chapter for understanding the subtleties of deeper meditative prayer experience.

At stake in this transition in our interior practice is a new level of surrender to God and the divine will. The method we practice is to surrender even our particular style of prayer. The methods of prayer with which we begin our deeper search into the interior are methods that our human mind employs. Thus, they are guided and directed by the human center of personality. They are very useful for training the human will and for learning interior discipline. But they can take us only to the threshold of deep knowledge of God, for God is beyond any method we can imagine. God communes with us also in ways beyond the words of our meditative prayer. Of course, Teresa is familiar with a wide range of such prayer methods, which we will discuss in chapter 3. In Mansions IV, the communication with God for which we have been longing begins to awaken. Our task, when we begin to be aware of this deeper interior Presence, is to let go of any formal prayer practice and attend to that Presence.

There is a profound and nonverbal level of surrender that we are asked to practice here. We are asked to let go of all of our agenda, no matter how well intentioned. We are asked to "surrender into the arms of love" (ibid., 331). When these moments of *infused prayer* or *gusto* or *spiritual delight* come, Teresa tells us that our task is to surrender to them. They often come at the beginning, only in brief moments. During these brief moments of absolute silence or light or heart-opening energy, our task is to learn to dwell in them, letting ourselves be bathed in love. She calls this stage the prayer of quiet. When the prayer of quiet awakens, we abandon our formal practice of recollection and abide with God. In these times of deep quiet the human will and the divine will are being "united" (ibid., 325). In these times, there also may be a suspension of the intellect or the internal words that often occupy our minds. "Let the soul enjoy [this experience] without any endeavors other than some loving words, for even though we may not try in this prayer to go without thinking of anything, I know that often the intellect will be suspended, even though for only a very brief moment" (ibid., 331).

The fact that this type of suspension of the intellect would be a sign of the deeper surrender of the human will to the divine will seems obvious when we reflect upon it. So much of our identity is supported by the perpetual internal self-talk of our minds. We are forever reflecting and naming our experience inwardly. We are perpetually liking and disliking the experience life presents to us. Imagine, then, surrendering all this internal barrage of self-identity into the no-thing-ness of God. Imagine surrendering our self-image, if only for a moment, into the unfathomable creativity of God. Imagine surrendering all our self-doubt, shame, and inward wounds, if for only a moment "into the arms of love." All of that, I think, is at stake in this profound surrender beyond words into the divine embrace. It is fascinating that Teresa notices the profound level of interior reorganization of the personality that is at stake in so simple a thing as suspending our ego voice, if for only moments at a time. She understands that this is an arena of profound inward healing, an arena in which the deepest splits of the personality are healed by the divine encounter of love. She realizes that "in this prayer the soul is not yet grown but is like a suckling child. If it turns away from its mother's breasts, what can be expected for it but death?" (ibid., 332). Teresa suggests that we are at the most primitive, even infant level of the psyche in these moments of deep suspension. A new life is being forged in this womb of prayer. She warns us not to turn away from this experience when it comes, but to begin the process of transformation it is bringing forth and attend to this process until its completion.

One of the most intriguing aspects of Mansions IV is Teresa's discussion of the physical sensations that accompany the prayer of quiet or moments of *gusto*. It is extremely rare in Western mystical literature to find such a complete description of the physical manifestations of spiritual awakening. A vast body of such literature exists in Eastern tradition, particularly in the Yogic tradition of Hinduism. There is also a strong contemporary interest in such physical activity that can accompany spiritual emergence (cf. Bragdon, 1990; Greenwell, 1990; Grof, 1990). In both the Hindu tradition and its contemporary manifestation, the physical phenomena that accompany spiritual awakening usually are termed *kundalini* experience. It is fascinating and instructive to see Teresa using physical phenomena to describe part of the subtle difference between *contentos* and *gustos*, the two types of spiritual experience that she elaborates in Mansions IV.

To describe the difference between *contentos* and *gustos*, Teresa quotes a psalm: "Cum dilatasti cor meum" (ibid., 318). The meaning of this psalm—"My heart is expanded, or exalted"— has the same intended meaning as the phrase in the Eucharist: "Lift up your hearts unto the Lord." For Teresa, this phrase, expanding the heart, is not a metaphor. It is an accurate description of a certain type of physical phenomenon that accompanies the experience of *gusto*. She says that the consolations, or *contentos*, do not expand the heart, but "constrain it a little" (ibid.).

She says that often, *contentos* are mixed with our own passions and can be accompanied by tears and "a tightening in the chest and even external bodily movements that [one] cannot restrain" (ibid., 322-23). These are the experiences often reported by the classical Hindu texts and contemporary persons who experience *kundalini* awakening. Contemporary bodywork disciplines also describe various kinds of physical shaking and releasing that can accompany deep relaxation, or the release of emotion triggered by the memory of a traumatic event in the past. Through the added insight provided by these contemporary theories, we can understand that Teresa probably is describing *contentos* as the arena of profound releasing of old memories and emotional patterns that have become located in the body. *Contentos* are experiences of physical and emotional release.

Gusto is an altogether different experience. Teresa says this seems to rise from a location other than the body, from the soul itself. Yet it also manifests in the body.

> To return to the verse, what I think is helpful in it for explaining this matter is the idea of expansion. It seems that since that heavenly water begins to rise from this spring I'm mentioning that is deep within us, it swells and expands our whole interior being, producing ineffable blessings; nor does the soul even understand what is given to it there. It perceives a fragrance, let us say for now, as though there were in that interior depth a brazier giving off sweet-smelling perfumes. No light is seen, nor is the place seen where the brazier is; but the warmth and the fragrant fumes spread through the entire soul and even often enough, as I have said, the body shares in them.... This spiritual delight is not something that can be imagined because however diligent our efforts we cannot acquire it. The very experience of it makes us realize that it is not of the same metal as we ourselves but fashioned from the purest gold of divine wisdom. Here, in my opinion, the faculties are not united but absorbed and looking as though in wonder at what they see. (Ibid., 324-25)

The image of water that she uses here is further elaborated. She says the experience of *contento* is like filling a trough with water that comes through an aqueduct and requires much ingenuity. When the experience of *gusto* is present, "the source of the water is right there, and the trough fills without any noise. If the spring is abundant, as is this one we are speaking about, the water overflows once the trough is filled, forming a large stream.... water is always flowing from the spring" (ibid., 323).

Teresa is aware that she is writing of extremely delicate matters. She makes the distinction between the absorption with the divine and what she calls a stupor. She reports a woman who thought she was absorbed in God and remained so eight hours at a time, to the point that she let herself become physically depleted. Such activity Teresa calls stupor and not *gusto*. Always speaking in practical ways, Teresa eschews such practice and suggests that if this *gusto* is genuine there will be "no languishing in the soul" (ibid., 334). Also, the genuine *gusto* lasts for a short time. The body does not weary. The person in such deep prayer may have a brief moment of absorption, then return to more discursive thought, and then again return to the experience of *gusto*. This alternation of experiences gives safety to the practice of deep surrender. Without it, one should be suspicious of the experience and seek counsel of a knowledgeable person.

MANSIONS V

This discussion is continued in Mansions V, although Teresa thinks that "it would be better not to say anything about these remaining rooms, for there is no way of knowing how to speak of them" (ibid., 335). Mansions V, however, elaborates not only the prayer experience, but gives extremely useful understandings of the ethical dimensions of this deep prayer, as well as imagery to assist in our receptivity to it.

She reminds us, as she has so frequently before, that there is need for perseverance. She speaks of this awareness of contemplative experience as being like enjoying heaven on earth (ibid., 336). We are enjoined to "dig until [the soul] finds this hidden treasure" (ibid.). In this chapter, she describes a deepening prayer of quiet that becomes the prayer of union, lasting up to a half hour (ibid., 343). During this time of deep union, there is such stillness that the body scarcely moves and there is very little breathing (ibid., 337). Sometimes in this prayer state, thoughts, memories, and imagination occur, but they do not disturb the profound inner silence.

Teresa eloquently returns to her theme of the will in Mansions V. She states that the union of human faculties mirrored in the silence of the prayer of union is the union of human and divine will and human and divine love. "For it is all a matter of love united with love, and the actions of love are most pure and so extremely delicate and gentle that there is no way of explaining them, but the Lord knows how to make them very clearly felt" (ibid., 354). During these periods of the prayer of union, the divine One who will eventually become spouse is secretly visiting. It is like a courtship. When God is fully present in the half-hour periods of union, the experience brings great happiness.

Now Teresa, in her characteristic fashion, is able to weave this attention to interior happiness and mystical silence into the praxis of daily life. She recalls again that the union in which we are engaged is a union of will with God. The test for the authenticity of our prayer is to notice whether we are growing in love for our neighbor. If we are not, then we are not yet at this level of surrender. She cites the possibility that a Sister of the convent would be willing to lay aside her contemplation to assist another Sister in need and, in fact, also find the experience of divine love in this active mode.

> [W]orks are what the Lord wants! He desires that if you see a Sister who is sick to whom you can bring some relief, you have compassion on her and not worry about losing this devotion; and that if she is suffering pain, you also feel it; and that, if necessary, you fast so that she might eat—not so much for her sake as because you know it is your Lord's desire. This is true union with His will, and if you see a person praised, the Lord wants you to be much happier than if you yourself were being praised. (Ibid., 352)

This comingling of a deepening prayer life with a more sensitive response to our neighbor signals for Teresa a truly new mode of life. In Mansions V, she introduces the metaphor of the silkworm and its transformation into a butterfly, as analogous to this profound transformation of the human being. In this metaphor, we also sense her extraordinary grasp of the possibilities of meditation on the mysteries of nature as leading us to the divine embrace. First, there is a little "seed," from which the silkworm comes forth. The growth of the silkworm she likens to our spiritual growth, when nurtured by "the remedies left by Him to His Church, by going to confession, reading good books, and hearing sermons" (ibid., 342). These are the methods Teresa cited in Mansions II as outward forms that enable our spiritual growth. Through these outward means, the silkworm is growing into maturity. Then Teresa likens our own meditation efforts as being like the silkworm spinning its cocoon. Through the efforts she described in Mansions III, we have created the cocoon for our "death," or transformation. Then, in the periods of profound silence, the butterfly emerges.

> When the soul is, in this prayer, truly dead to the world, a little white butterfly comes forth. Oh, greatness of God! How transformed the soul is when it comes out of this prayer after having been placed within the greatness of God and so closely joined with Him for a little while—in my opinion the union never lasts for as much as a half hour. Truly, I tell you that the soul doesn't recognize itself. Look at the difference between an ugly worm and a little white butterfly; that's what the difference is here. (Ibid.)

This difference also creates its own suffering for the individual. Embracing God and being embraced by God are experiences so fulfilling that all else pales in contrast. Matters of earthly life may become very painful, particularly in regard to people who seem to be living at such a great distance from the divine. Teresa seems to accept this type of suffering as an inevitable consequence of the deepening surrender. She continues also to call for renewed attention to the surrender of human will to divine will. That surrender becomes the ballast to enable the individual to deal with this struggle for understanding and appropriation of the great gifts of the experiences of divine union. She also grounds this experience in the world of nature, by suggesting that we meditate on the transformation of the silkworm into the butterfly as our meditation practice.

This is enough, Sisters, for a period of meditation even though I may say no more to you; in it you can consider the wonders and the wisdom of our God. Well now, what would happen if we knew the property of every created thing. It is very beneficial for us to busy ourselves thinking of these grandeurs and delighting in being brides of a King so wise and powerful. (Ibid., 342)

Teresa reinforces the profound nature of this transformation: "[T]ake careful note, daughters, that it is necessary for the silkworm to die, and moreover, at a cost to yourselves" (ibid., 350).

MANSIONS VI

In Mansions VI, Teresa continues this discussion, giving considerable detail to interior states of prayer and the process of discernment. The discussion of these issues is found in chapter 4, which will give attention to spiritual experience and discernment. The heart of the material for chapter 4 comes from Teresa's Mansions VI.

In describing the deepening prayer of Teresa, it is sufficient to point out the intensification of experience in Mansions VI. This intensification is both in the nature of suffering and in the various ecstasies of prayer. Teresa does not herself use the term "dark night of the soul." However, if we look at her description of Mansions VI, it appears to follow the pattern reported by others who have made the deepest journey of surrender into God. Evelyn Underhill, in describing the pattern of Western mysticism, spoke of a five-stage model for spiritual development. These levels are: awakening of the self; purification of the self; illumination of the self; dark night of the soul; and the unitive way (1961). Underhill's pattern is illuminative of Teresa's Mansions. Her Mansions I and II have to do with awakening of the self to a deeper life with God. Mansions III and the experiences of *contentos* in Mansions IV might well be described as purification processes. The experiences of *gustos*, the prayer of quiet, and the prayer of union are experiences of illumination.

It is intriguing to note that for Underhill, the deepening prayer life leads to a final and deeper purification process which she describes as the dark night of the soul. Teresa's Mansions VI contains much material that suggests such a deep-level purification.

Teresa speaks in Mansions VI of the "tempest" of the mind, counterposed by the "consolation" given like the sunlight to the soul (Kavanaugh and Rodriguez, 1980, 364). The key point for Teresa in this period of severe testing is that one's own efforts bear little fruit, while more and more one is utterly dependent upon divine grace. The mental tempests come upon one, only to be suddenly lifted by a moment of divine clarity. It even seems that the soul is abandoned and that "grace is so hidden . . . that not even a very tiny spark is visible" (ibid., 364-5). It is a time when solitude and mental prayer provide very little consolation, and indeed may bring greater despair. It is also a time when, if one is given to illness, the torment of the body may become even more extreme (ibid., 362). In addition to these interior trials, Teresa elaborates on exterior trials that may come. People do not understand the dynamics of this deep transformation, and so may ridicule the person undergoing such interior trials. Very often, poor spiritual direction is given.

These trials are exacerbated by the exquisite love the soul experiences in times of intimacy with God. Because these times of deep union are fleeting, the individual is left languishing for a full union with God.

> The soul desires to be completely occupied in love and does not want to be taken up with anything else, but to be so occupied is impossible for it even though it may want to; for although the will is not dead, the fire that usually makes it burn is dying out, and someone must necessarily blow on the fire so that heat will be given off. (Ibid., 400)

This combination of divine presence and absence makes the soul feel that "it is wounded in the most exquisite way" (ibid., 367). The way the individual keeps her balance through these interior trials is to "engage in external works of charity and to hope in the mercy of God who never fails those who hope in Him" (ibid., 365).

If we place these spiritual trials and sufferings in the context of Teresa's notion of final union being a union of the divine and human will, then we can understand the depth of "dying" that the human will must endure. Indeed, in describing the final union, Teresa returns to the metaphor of the butterfly, stating that the butterfly dies.

There are two types of union for Teresa. In the lesser type, union is like the joining of the flames of two lighted candles. They can be separated again. However, the final union is like rain falling into a stream, or two beams of sunlight coming through two different windows and crossing each other. In those types of union, there is an essence that no longer can be separated (ibid., 434). That is the final union of human and divine will, of human and divine personality, that Teresa discovers. For that union to manifest, there is such a surrender required of the human will that every moment of increasing surrender is perceived as suffering. And every moment of separation from full divine love is perceived as suffering. In short, this final purification of the self requires a final surrender of all self-bound motivations, with an awakening to the divine source within.

While Teresa describes these deep shifts of the personality in Mansions VI, she also gives her most elaborate descriptions of unusual spiritual experiences. Simultaneously, the soul is relinquishing its sense-bound modes of perception and awakening to its deepest intuitive capacities. Throughout this intensified spiritual experience, God sends "this action of love" that is like "a whisper so penetrating that the soul cannot help but hear it" (ibid., 367). Among the spiritual experiences Teresa describes here are locutions or interior words that seem to be spoken by God (ibid., 372); interior visions (ibid., 380); such quiet that the body becomes cold and breathing seems almost to cease (ibid., 384); out-of-body experiences (ibid., 388); and speaking in tongues (ibid., 395). As I have indicated, we will discuss these phenomena in chapter 4. Here it is important to point out the central theme for Teresa. None of these experiences is sought out by the individual. They may or may not come to any particular person. The sign that they are authentic is that they bring one into an ever more lasting sense of divine love and that they bring forth trustworthy guidance for increased interior knowledge and exterior service.

MANSIONS VII

All this heightened psychic experience and surrender manifests finally in a full union with God. In Mansions VI, betrothal is assured. In Mansions VII, the interior marriage is actualized. For Teresa, this interior marriage occurred through a vision of the Holy Trinity, with the simultaneous inward conviction that the union of wills had taken place. As described earlier in this chapter, Teresa's Trinity is a Trinity of active charity, with an awakening of inward charity and outward resolve. Not surprisingly, then, she concludes that the purpose of this spiritual marriage is "the birth always of good works, good works" (ibid., 446). "In sum, my Sisters, what I conclude with is that we shouldn't build castles in the air. The Lord doesn't look so much at the greatness of our works as at the love with which they are done" (ibid., 450).

Thus, we have a masterful conclusion of the pathway that brings a divided self together. The union of human will, motivations, and faculties, with the divine center is complete. Henceforth, one has the sense that the recipient of this spiritual marriage is in fact serene. It is intriguing that Teresa gives little attention to interior experiences in Mansions VII. Here, attention turns outward again. The mistress of the interior has shown herself to be finally concerned with the life of active love within the world. But the human will has proven formidable, pressed first into service to help discern the whispers of love within the human heart where God resides, then learning to surrender fully to the messages of this deep interior. Committing herself to undertake this absolute surrender to God has given Teresa not only an awakened divine soul but a human soul of greatness.

Exercises for Reflection and Prayer

1. As you read the description of Teresa's Mansions, is there one of the Mansions that "feels" more familiar to you than the others? The intent of the Mansions is not to describe an exact location for your spiritual life, but rather to point in the general direction of your spiritual development. In what ways does Teresa's description of spiritual life and practice within that Mansions relate to your experience?

Mansions I: Little light for the interior presence of God. Very concerned with worldly matters.

Mansions II: Dependent upon external means for remembering God, but availing oneself of those things: good sermons, regular worship, good books, supportive conversation.

Mansions III: Undertaking discipline of prayer, self-reflection, and active charity.

Mansions IV: Moments of quiet begin to come during meditative prayer.

Mansions V: Prayer of union, with deep experiences of inner teaching from God or inner healing. May be emotionally difficult as deep inner feelings and inner wounds are addressed.

Mansions VI: Much interior exploration of inner prayer experiences. God teaching from deep within. God transforming the personality through new insights, deep healing experiences. Sense that union with God will come.

Mansions VII: Life lived in sense of continual union between God and yourself. Life is "simple," in that you act on God's guid-

ance without inner conflict. Life lived in grace of ongoing deeds of charity inspired by God.

2. Another way to understand Teresa's description of the seven Mansions is to understand that our life is a spiritual pilgrimage with many changes, both in our ways of praying and in the kinds of personal concerns that are foremost for us at a given time. Write a spiritual autobiography of approximately 3 to 5 pages. Think about significant events in your spiritual development. Describe the different ways you have related to God through the years. Note these. What people have been your spiritual friends, guides, or have posed spiritual challenges to you? You might prefer to draw your spiritual pilgrimage as a path. It can also be illuminating to draw your spiritual pilgrimage as a graph with "highs" and "lows" noted, together with their intensity. Use colors.

3. Describe your most natural mode of prayer. It may be intercession; it may be praise; it may be meditation. Perhaps you have experienced "moments" of the prayer of quiet or union that Teresa describes. Perhaps your most prayerful times occur while walking in nature.

4. Do you have a particular way of addressing or naming God that is most comfortable in prayer? Do you find your address of God changing from time to time?

5. Describe within your own life an understanding of the concept of aligning the human will with the divine will.

CHAPTER THREE
Praying with Teresa

A soul hidden in God,
What has it to desire
Save to love more and more,
And, in love all hidden
Again and again to love You?
One all possessing love I ask
My God, my soul centered in You,
Making a delightful nest,
A resting place most pleasing.

From "Loving Colloquy" (Vol. 3, 380),
The Collected Works of St. Teresa of Avila

s we approach Teresian prayer, we will follow her own division of deep prayer and describe three types of meditative prayer experience: the prayer of recollection; the prayer of quiet; and the prayer of union. These terms represent degrees of penetration into divine mystery, beginning with a style of meditative prayer in which our minds are quite active and ending in profound silence, in which we become utterly receptive to God's messages to us.

Underlying this development toward silence is the deepening relationship between the interior God and our surface-level motivations and self-understandings. In the previous chapter, we described Teresa's understanding of that interior movement

77

through the seven Mansions. As we begin this discussion of her methods of prayer, let us explore another of the images she used to describe the levels of prayer. This image of the stages of prayer appears in her *Life*. She likens our spiritual development to the cultivation of a garden. We begin with barren soil, full of weeds. God pulls the weeds and plants the seeds, but our part is to cultivate the garden. Teresa speaks of the way we water the garden with metaphors describing the various types of prayer:

> You may draw water from a well (which is for us a lot of work). Or you may get it by means of a water wheel and aqueducts in such a way that it is obtained by turning the crank of the water wheel. (I have drawn it this way sometimes—the method involves less work than the other, and you get more water). Or it may flow from a river or a stream. (The garden is watered much better by this means because the ground is more fully soaked, and there is no need to water so frequently—and much less work for the gardener.) Or the water may be provided by a great deal of rain. (For the Lord waters the garden without any work on our part—and this way is incomparably better than all the others mentioned.) (Kavanaugh and Rodriguez, 1976, 80-81)

Teresa will thus guide us toward a state of sublime surrender to God, where in silence we will be taught in an interior way. In proposing this fourfold deepening in silence, Teresa reflects her personal experience in meditative prayer and proposes a model for practicing surrender of our will to God. In addition, this model reflects the collective wisdom of the Western mystical pathway. In her own way, Teresa describes a dynamic similar to the fourfold pattern of meditative prayer suggested in the Benedictine formula for meditating on scripture: Reading, Meditating, Prayer, Contemplation. Both Teresa's mode of prayer and the Benedictine model begin with the exertion of our own capacities for attention and training of the human will within the human psyche and end in a state of sublime silence.

Teresa's fourfold metaphor for watering the garden relates to the threefold pattern of prayer of recollection, prayer of quiet, prayer of union. She states that the prayer of recollection is like our watering the garden by drawing water from the well. It takes a great deal of personal effort to effect this prayer. The use of the crank to turn the water wheel represents the first degree of the prayer of quiet. The watering of the field by the stream represents a deeper experience of the prayer of quiet. Finally, when the field is simply watered by rain falling from the sky on its own, we have experienced the prayer of union. Teresian prayer teaches us an interior mode of surrender and an interior way of listening for divine guidance. It begins with technique and ends in the abandonment of the human self into the divine "arms of love" (Kavanaugh and Rodriguez, 1980, 331).

PRAYER OF RECOLLECTION

The prayer of recollection is the basic term used in Teresa's time for meditative prayer that involves some technique. It was used to describe a wide range of practices. Teresa speaks of meditating on scripture, meditating on images of Christ or other holy visage, and meditating on images that come spontaneously from her own psyche, such as the interior castle. For Teresa this type of meditative prayer is intensely relational: "[S]peak with [God] as you would with a father, or a brother, or a lord, or as with a spouse; sometimes in one way, at other times in another; He will teach you what you must do in order to please Him. . . . This prayer is called 'recollection,' because the soul collects its faculties together and enters within itself to be with its God" (Kavanaugh and Rodriguez, 1980, 141). Recollection calls us into a certain kind of attention within ourselves.

Teresa uses the term *faculties* to mean all the human attributes through which I engage myself with the world. These faculties are the senses, reason, imagination, and feelings. They are intended to be the guardians of the great interior of my soul, but when I begin to enter into awareness of myself, I usually find that there is great internal quarreling among these faculties. For example, my feelings may be quarreling with my

79

self-concept. I may find myself saying, I "want" and quickly countering with, "but you shouldn't think that." Or I am thinking some interesting thoughts, and a loud sound interrupts from the environment. I listen for a moment and completely forget what I was thinking. It is the function of these human faculties to take in a great deal of information outwardly and inwardly, in order to give me what I need to function effectively in the world. However, they often can vie for supremacy because I do not realize that there is a divine center within me, seeking to give direction to the totality. There is a divine will. It resides within me and seeks to direct my whole being, but my faculties, such as my senses and my imagination, don't realize that there is the possibility of unified action in the service of a greater good. Instead, they are forever quarreling with one another.

One of the great works you do as you learn the process of recollection is to notice and learn to exercise some control over the wild bramble of your interior faculties. The term *recollection* has wonderful connotations. It has the connotation of re-collecting yourself—that is, bringing the many disparate functions into a semblance of order. It contains the notion of collecting your whole being together. Think of the description of the man in scripture who called himself Legion, because there were so many of him (Mark 5). Your multiple interior functions also have the natural capability of being in conflict with one another. As you "collect" yourself together, you naturally experience a new capacity for serenity and interior cooperation. You also train each faculty not to have its own way all the time. And you learn to give due respect to all your faculties, feelings as well as reason, imagination as well as sensations. The multiple interior capacities learn to cooperate for good.

The term *recollection* also has the connotation of remembering. In this respect, it is much like the sense of remembrance in the Eucharist. Jesus' phrase during the last supper, "Do this in remembrance of me," has an intriguing meaning in Greek. *Anamnesis*, the Greek word for remembering, literally means to remember again. *Anamnesis* is thus to stop forgetting and reclaim our memory of Christ. Teresa's use of "recollection" has much the same meaning. She invites us to stop living, as if our whole life is an internal chaos of conflicting drives and forces, and to stop forgetting that within the living center of each of us God resides in radiant splendor, seeking to direct us toward loving action in all our endeavors. Thus, she speaks of the positive results of the prayer of recollection:

> Through the prayer of recollection, the soul's divine Master comes more quickly to teach it and give it the prayer of quiet than He would through any other method it might use.... Those who by such a method can enclose themselves within this little heaven of our soul, where the Maker of heaven and earth is present, and grow accustomed to refusing to be where the exterior senses in their distraction have gone or look in that direction should believe they are following an excellent path and that they will not fail to drink water from the fount; for they will journey far in a short time. (Ibid., 141-42)

Journeying far in a short time is made possible not only by the content of the prayer of recollection but by the process itself. In terms of content, any holy thought or image will assist us to focus our attention. It is useful to remember that in Teresa's discussion of the *Interior Castle*, she speaks of the utilization of the prayer of recollection in Mansions III. This is the arena of learning discipline. The prayer of recollection enables us to learn a kind of discipline of the mind, so that we can begin to distinguish the multitude of interior voices and learn to listen for the divine voice. After we have explored a few more of Teresa's comments regarding the prayer, I will offer some examples of her meditative style of recollection using different forms. All these various forms have some direct reference in her writings. After these examples, we will turn to a discussion of the prayer of quiet and the prayer of union.

Teresa advises us to focus our attention on the interior awareness we are seeking—approaching God in relationship. Though she utilizes many different forms, the key to the prayer of recollection is to use our human capacities to aim our awareness toward divine love. "The fire of divine love is more quickly

81

enkindled when [we] blow a little with [our] intellects" (ibid., 143). This "blowing a little with the intellect" refers to the use of particular images or meditation forms. In this specific example, she is talking about the use of an image as the meditation focus. Notice, however, that the intent is a deep communion with the living divine force within ourselves.

Teresa suggests that we should not seek to resist our stream of thoughts. In several places in her writings, she comments that even when we are very absorbed in interior quiet, it may be that we will notice that the mind is still busy. She encourages us not to pay attention to that quality of the mind, but to use our method of recollection to place ourselves in the divine presence. In this advice she mirrors other practitioners of meditation and meditative prayer, who suggest that we not try to block ourselves from a particular type of interior awareness, for to do so usually creates interior turmoil, rather than success. However, if we draw ourselves toward that which is greater, we will eventually discern the greatness of God calling back to us.

Put in simple terms, the qualities of interior experience that we access during meditative prayer may be diagrammed as shown in chart 1. See Appendix for additional information.

During our experiences of meditative prayer, we journey from the surface level awareness toward this deep interior quiet in the arena of ultimate awareness. And according to Teresa, there is a movement initiated by God from these depths toward our surface-level awareness.

The prayer of recollection begins with turning our attention toward the ultimate, within, and then we begin to notice that God is seeking to access our surface-level awareness as well. There is a genuine two-way communication underway in this process. Thus, in Teresa's understanding, not only do we reach toward God within our deep interior, but God is simultaneously reaching out toward us from our depths, seeking to influence our thinking, our emotions, and our exterior actions.

As the prayer of recollection directs us toward the divine presence and will, we learn more receptivity to that presence. This receptivity is manifest in times of quiet. "When His Majesty desires the intellect to stop, He occupies it in another way and

CHART 1

EXTERIOR WORLD

- -

INTERIOR WORLD

SURFACE LEVEL AWARENESS:

Sensory awareness / Discursive thinking / Ordinary mental process

- -

SYMBOLIC LEVEL AWARENESS:

Imagination/Imagery as tool to deeper quiet/Emotional awareness

- -

ULTIMATE AWARENESS:

God "enthroned on the heart"/Divine "arms of love"
Experiences of being taught by God in deep silence

gives it a light so far above what we can attain that it remains absorbed. Then, without knowing how, the intellect is much better instructed than it was through all the soul's efforts not to make use of it" (Kavanaugh and Rodriguez, 1980, 330).

We will have more to say about this process when we speak of the prayer of quiet, but here it is useful to gain an understanding of the interior dynamic that Teresa describes during the experience of meditative prayer.

During the prayer of recollection, the human will is directing its attention toward the divine center. By our own efforts, we seek to bridle our busy minds and attend to God. Through our human effort, training and directing ourselves toward the divine center, we also become less distracted by external concerns. An effort of human will is required here, as well as the learning of an interior surrender to discern divine presence and guidance.

The symbolic level of awareness plays an important role in assisting us to discern God within. Imagery and emotional awareness form a bridge through which the surface and the ultimate levels of interior experience communicate with each other. Teresa was especially gifted in using this imaginative quality of the mind, as we will see in exploring the prayer forms. In the midst of our efforts to refine the quality of our attention, moments of the prayer of quiet arise. During those times of profound quiet, God breaks through to our surface level awareness, cleansing and redeeming our emotions and deep motivations in the process. We are left with a sense of sweetness and divine presence.

During the prayer of union, there is such a profound breakthrough to the divine presence that, ultimately, the distinctions between surface and deep level awareness dissolves, and we simply express the divine will into the world.

With this understanding of the interior dynamics of meditative prayer, let us turn to particular forms of the prayer of recollection taught by Teresa. My intent is to offer a manual on prayer. Each prayer form will be presented with guidance, so that it can be used for meditation. Each form will begin with directions to assist us in setting ourselves within the attitude of recollection.

In particular, we will explore meditative prayer on the relationship with God, with a divine image, with the imagery of the interior castle, with discursive reading of scripture or other wisdom literature, with imaginative use of scripture, and meditating on the processes of nature.

RECOLLECTION THROUGH RELATIONSHIP WITH GOD

This form of meditative prayer is, in many ways, the most pivotal for Teresa, I believe. Her intent is that we experience a living relationship with the divine presence within ourselves. Her meditative practice is built on this relationship. She calls this interior presence by many attributes, sometimes referring to God as His Majesty, Guest, father, brother, lord, spouse (ibid., 140-41). She encourages us to speak with God "sometimes in one way, at other times in another" (ibid., 141). She has a very lively relationship with Christ, as well, so she often approaches the divine through Christ. In one of her rapturous writings, she speaks of being sustained by the divine breasts: "For from those divine breasts where it seems God is always sustaining the soul there flow streams of milk bringing comfort to all the people of the castle" (ibid., 435). Thus, I think, she also would be comfortable approaching God in feminine forms, as well as masculine.

Within the varieties of address toward God, the key for Teresa is that we not resist the relationship with God. She writes very graphically of the wrong kind of humility, a humility through which we refuse to entertain the notion that God is truly present within us and available to us. In the eloquent chapter 28 of *The Way of Perfection*, she writes:

Leave aside any of that faintheartedness that some persons have and think is humility. You see, humility doesn't consist in refusing a favor the King offers you but in accepting such a favor and understanding how bountifully it comes to you and being delighted with it. What a nice kind of humility! I have the Emperor of heaven and earth in my house (for He comes to it in order to favor me and be happy with me), and out of humility I do not want to answer Him or stay with Him or take what He gives me, but I leave Him alone. Or, while He is telling me and begging me to ask Him for something, I do not do so but remain poor; and I even let Him go, for He sees that I never finish trying to make up my mind.

Have nothing to do with this kind of humility, daughters, but speak with Him as with a father, or a brother, or a lord, or as with a spouse; sometimes in one way, at other times in another; He will teach you what you must do in order to please Him. Don't be foolish; take Him at His word. Since He is your Spouse, He will treat you accordingly. (Ibid., 141)

God is accessible to us through the practice of the prayer of recollection.

You already know that God is everywhere. It's obvious, then, that where the king is there is his court; in sum, wherever God is, there is heaven. Without a doubt you can believe that where His Majesty is present, all glory is present. Consider what St. Augustine says, that he sought Him in many places but found Him ultimately within himself. Do you think it matters little for a soul with a wandering mind to understand this truth and see that there is no need to go to heaven in order to speak with one's Eternal Father or find delight in Him? Nor is there any need to shout. However softly we speak, He is near enough to hear us. Neither is there any need for wings to go to find Him. All one need do is go into solitude and look at Him within oneself, and not turn away from so good a Guest but with great humility speak to Him as to a father. (Ibid., 140-41)

Teresa concludes this marvelous chapter with the following observation:

For, in my opinion, if I had understood as I do now that in this little palace of my soul dwelt so great a King, I would not have

86

left Him alone so often. . . . But what a marvelous thing, that He who would fill a thousand worlds and many more with His grandeur would enclose Himself in something so small! [And so He wanted to enclose Himself in the womb of His most Blessed Mother.] In fact, since He is Lord He is free to do what He wants, and since He loves us He adapts Himself to our size. (Ibid., 144)

With this introduction to her intensely relational understanding of meditative prayer, let us turn to an experience of this relationship in the style of the prayer of recollection.

As you prepare yourself for this experience, find a comfortable chair for sitting with back straight, or you may sit on the floor, with a cushion sufficiently high to allow your back to be straight and your legs relaxed. As with all of Teresa's meditations, it is also wonderful to practice them as she often did, in a chapel. Or you may want to arrange a place in your home with religious significance for you, perhaps lighting a candle or arranging a small altar. Once you have your place and your position arranged, practice the principle of recollection by turning your attention inward. An excellent way to begin is to be aware of your breathing within your chest and abdomen. Spend a few moments being aware of the rising and falling of your body with your breathing. Notice that even in a short time, your attention will alternate between being very focused on your breathing and then wandering off in other directions. This is the nature of the surface-level mind. Its task is to bring as much into our awareness as it can.

However, the principle of recollection is that when we notice that our mind is wandering, we gently bring it back to the primary focus of the meditation. This is a practice of will. This is the principle of recollection in which we seek to train ourselves toward giving attention to matters of ultimate meaning and learn to distinguish our awareness from frivolous, self-defeating, or hurtful interior thinking

87

patterns. It is very helpful in this process to remember Teresa's instruction—do not try to stop a thought, but instead, turn our attention toward the divine Guest within ourselves. In other words, we allow our thoughts to be influenced by the great thought, that within us and accessible to us lies the divine source of life and love.

As you turn your attention inward toward the divine Center, ask yourself what term you would give today to the quality of your relationship with God. Find a term you like. You might try some of the terms in Teresa's descriptions of her relationship with God: father, mother, guest, emperor of heaven and earth, brother, lord, spouse, Christ. Or use another term: friend, companion, creator, healer, teacher, to name a few. Find one particular term, and then mentally repeat that term softly as you turn your attention inward toward the divine presence.

Again, do not try to suppress your wandering mind. It is nearly impossible to do so. Also, we want an open mind to be available for inward teaching, intuitions, and insights to arise. However, if you find that your mind is wandering very far from its attention to God, then gently bring your awareness back to the term of relationship with which you are working and renew your prayer. Remember that Teresa's imagery places this divine presence at the heart. So it also can be useful to continue the awareness of breathing focused in the trunk of the body, as a way to keep our attention present to all dimensions of ourselves, physical and emotional, as well as mental.

As you practice this prayer of relationship, be attentive to the inner invitation to become very simple, to let a single word emerge as the meditation focus. Notice subtle shifts in breathing and energy that quiet your mind and emotions. Be alert to the interior summons of God to speak your mind and heart to God simply, laying out your concerns, but also being available for new understandings to emerge.

PRAYER OF RECOLLECTION ON A HOLY IMAGE

Carry about an image or painting of this Lord that is to your liking, not so as to carry it about on your heart and never look at it but so as to speak often with Him; for He will inspire you with what to say. Since you speak with other persons, why must words fail you more when you speak with God? Don't believe they will; at least I will not believe they will if you acquire the habit. (Ibid., 136)

Teresa invites us into relationship with Christ through the use of a visual image. She reflects a well-developed imaginative method of recollective prayer of her time in recommending this practice. Teresa was very clear about the power of image to stir the heart toward God. Notice how gentle her comments are, however: "Pick an image that you like." And then talk with this image as if you are speaking directly to God. Engage in relationship with God as you would with another person. She encourages us to let go of the intellect with its questions and discursive ponderings, and instead approach Christ through our own emotional state at a given time. "I'm not asking you now that you think about Him or that you draw out a lot of concepts or make long and subtle reflections with your intellect. I'm not asking you to do anything more than look at Him" (ibid., 33-34).

She then comments that we should direct our imagination toward an image of Christ's life that reflects our current situation: "If you are joyful, look at Him as risen. . . . If you are experiencing trials or are sad, behold Him on the way to the garden: what great affliction He bore in His soul; for having become suffering itself . . . . Or behold Him burdened with the cross" (ibid., 134). We note throughout her comments the intimacy with which she addresses Christ as her spouse, a spouse who is fully present to her in whatever human state she finds herself.

In fact, Teresa turns around the convention of her day, in which it was expected that the wife adjust her mood to suit that of her husband. Teresa states, instead, that Christ adjusts to our moods and meets us exactly as we are. "See what subjection you have been freed from, Sisters!" she writes, commenting on the liberty of women in the convent at that time, as opposed to those who were married (ibid.). There is something profoundly healing in this approach. We are invited to be absolutely present to our own current situation and not wish our internal state to be different. However, Teresa finds in Christ a companion whose range of emotional life mirrors precisely each of these states within us, and thus elevates us toward a divine understanding of the circumstances that are influencing us.

Notice that this form of meditative presence to the divine image may take place at any time. It is not necessarily limited to a formal time for prayer and reflection. Rather, if you have a small image that you can carry with you, take it out from time to time and ponder God as manifest in this image. Or there may be a particular image within a place of worship toward which you can focus your prayer. Teresa would encourage us to look for artworks or artifacts that transport us toward the divine image, to give us a vehicle to engage our imagination and our emotions. This image could be of Christ, as it is for Teresa, or of Mary. Find an image, Teresa writes, "that you like." In this practice, Teresa appeals to the simplicity of the human heart and its image-making capacity.

Many years ago, I visited a small cathedral in Mexico. On the wall was a great mural, in which Christ, Mary, and the Apostles were located at the top. At the lowest level was humanity, exhibiting a myriad of forms of misfortune and struggle. Many were reaching up toward divine help. In between the divine and the human realms were the saints, lending their assistance to the struggling people. Teresa encourages such visual representations of divine assistance. We must remember that she wrote in large measure for women who did not read. She knew the power of image to convey deep meaning, and she knew the limitations of rationality. We notice how attuned her style of recollection is to human emotional needs.

If you would like to practice this method and do not have a particular image with which to work, you still may do so. We will begin again with the instructions for the prayer of recollection on relationship with God, and then modify them in order to suggest a way to work with image.

As you prepare yourself for this experience, find a comfortable chair for sitting with back straight, or you may sit on the floor, with a cushion sufficiently high to allow your back to be straight and your legs relaxed. If you have an image with which you wish to meditate, place it before you, so that you can look at it directly from time to time. If you do not have an image, we will be inviting our imagination to give us an image in this time of reflective prayer. Once you have your place and your position arranged, practice the principle of recollection by turning your attention inward. An excellent way to begin is to be aware of your breathing within your chest and abdomen. Spend a few moments being aware of the rising and falling of your body with your breathing.

As you turn your attention inward toward the divine Center, ask yourself what you are feeling today. What are the emotions that are uppermost on your heart? What situations of concern are present to you today? Or what experiences of delight and joy are present to you? Then, ask yourself for an image of God to assist you today, to help you to be fully present to yourself, as well as fully present to God. Remember the great variety of terms for God that Teresa has suggested. Perhaps God will be present as Holy Spirit, or as Divine Mother, or as Holy Father, or as Christ. Imagine that this divine One truly shares your concerns and your life in this moment. Or if you have an image before you, ponder your life concerns before this image.

You also can return to the instructions on recollection through relationship with God. What term would you give today to the quality of your relationship with God? Find a term you like. You might consider some of the terms in Teresa's descriptions of her relationship with God: father, mother, guest, emperor of heaven and earth, brother, lord, spouse, Christ. Or use another term: friend, companion, creator, healer, teacher, to name a few. Find one particular term, and then mentally repeat that term softly as you turn your attention inward toward the divine presence. Then, invite your imagination to give you an image of this divine presence and offer your prayers and concerns through this image to God.

Be fully present to yourself. Do not try to suppress your wandering mind or emotions. However, if you find that your mind is straying very far from its attention to God, gently bring your awareness back to the image and the term of relationship with which you are working, and renew your prayer.

Again, be present to the possibility of simplicity emerging. This prayer form is quite evocative emotionally. However, as you pray the prayer, you may receive insights and clarifications that resolve your emotional concerns. When that happens, do not resist the help that comes.

When you have become somewhat proficient in this form of imaging, it can be a very powerful method for prayers of inner healing and healing of memories. If deeply wounding circumstances from your past or present come to mind, this way of offering ourselves for healing can be very beneficial. Bring those concerns before God and pray to God through the image that is before you. Offer your life for blessing and healing. Be willing to forgive and be made whole again. If a memory of a wounding experience comes to mind, bring Christ into the experience in your imagination. It can be enormously freeing to experience God's healing presence in a situation in which a wound is held in our memory. We would follow Teresa's advice here, simply to gaze upon the Lord in this situation. Great benefit can come, often in surprising ways.

RECOLLECTION WITH THE INTERIOR CASTLE

Well, let us imagine that within us is an extremely rich palace, built entirely of gold and precious stones; in sum, built for a lord such as this. Imagine, too, as is indeed so, that you have a part to play in order for the palace to be so beautiful; for there is no edifice as beautiful as is a soul pure and full of virtues. The greater the virtues the more resplendent the jewels. Imagine, also, that in this palace dwells this mighty King who has been gracious enough to become your Father; and that He is seated upon an extremely valuable throne, which is your heart.

This may seem trifling at the beginning; I mean, this image I've used in order to explain recollection. But the image may be very helpful—to you especially—for since we women have no learning, all of this imagining is necessary that we may truly understand that within us lies something incomparably more precious than what we see outside ourselves. Let's not imagine that we are hollow inside. (Ibid., 143-44)

In this powerful image from *The Way of Perfection*, Teresa anticipates the imagery of her later writing, *Interior Castle*. She suggests that we use this image of the interior palace, or castle, as a meditation tool. It is very important to notice that this image is from Teresa's own reflection. While the image is referenced in Scripture, the power of the image to teach us about God came to Teresa during her own meditation.

I take from Teresa's example a tremendous liberty for us each to allow the deeper stirrings of the creative imagination to give us personal images that speak of the divine center of the human being. I have been impressed in teaching this material by how many people have had such an experience in their own spiritual pilgrimage. One woman told of a particular image of Christ's hands that arose in meditation during a time of intense crisis in her life when one of her children almost died. That form of meditative presence of Christ sustained her for many years and became her usual image for prayer. After those years, however, it ceased to convey power to her, and she found her meditation form changing. My point is that here is one of the most empowering forms of meditation that we receive from Teresa. By example, she encourages us to look for and honor those deep symbolic images within our own psyche.

This image of the interior palace, or castle, is represented sometimes in her other writings as a diamond or crystal, from which the presence of God emanates as brilliant light (see Revelation 21). "The brilliance of this inner vision is like that of an infused light coming from a sun covered by something as transparent as a properly cut diamond" (ibid., 412). One of her great revelations was that this light shining through the diamond was always present, seeking to give light and direction to the whole interior, but sin was represented as a black cloth or tar covering the diamond, so that light could not get out. Our task in cultivating the prayer of recollection is to do our part to lift the veil of misunderstanding that lies between ourselves and the great interior presence of God. When she speaks of the virtues as assisting us, she means that we should do our own part to cultivate a life of active love toward our fellow human beings.

As you prepare yourself to practice the prayer of recollection with this image, find a comfortable chair for sitting with back straight, or you may sit on the floor, with a cushion sufficiently high to allow your back to be straight and your legs relaxed. Once you have your place and your position arranged, practice the principle of recollection by simply turning your attention inward. Begin by being aware of your breathing within your chest and abdomen. Spend a few moments being aware of the rising and falling of your body with your breathing. As you turn your attention inward toward the divine Center, invite your imagination to give you an image of the interior palace or castle resplendent with jewels and gold, or invite an image of the interior diamond or crystal. Let light emanate from the center, bringing divine blessing, love, and insight to all that it touches.

You may want to personalize this image by incorporating a quality of relationship to God within your meditation, or drawing in a more personal image of God from the two previous forms of recollection I have described. The intention here is to be present to God through the image. If words describing this relationship assist your focus, use them. But primarily, this is a practice in presence to the divine light refracted out of the deep interior.

In teaching this method, I have found that many people are quite delighted to find this form, and the diamond or crystal speaks very directly to them. For others, I have found the diamond, crystal, or palace seems too cold and distant. Let yourself begin with Teresa's image, but be open to another image emerging that conveys your understanding of divine presence and guidance. More than once, I have heard people report that the image shifted to a flower. The gentle image of a living, growing, plant was more descriptive than the diamond at the time of these persons' current inner needs. Often people have found great benefit from meditating on the inner diamond, crystal, or palace, and have expressed their gratitude for this image.

Be fully present to yourself. Do not try to suppress your wandering mind or emotions. However, if you find that your mind is straying very far from its attention to God, then gently bring your awareness back to the image and term of relationship with which you are working, and renew your prayer.

Again, be present to the possibility of simplicity emerging. This prayer form can be conducive to moments of the emerging prayer of quiet, when God quiets the intellect with light. If this experience comes, be open to it.

RECOLLECTION ON
A SACRED WORD OR PHRASE

One of the primary roots of Christian spiritual development is a relationship with Scripture. Teresa's prayer assumes an intimate relationship with God developed by praying through the words of Scripture. In *The Way of Perfection*, she describes scriptural and nonscriptural sources for inspiring words or phrases to facilitate our prayer of recollection. She cites the use of the Lord's Prayer and the Hail Mary, both found in Scripture, as very sure methods for recollection in prayer (ibid., 118). She is fond of the words of the Gospels as a source of inspiration leading to recollection (ibid., 118).

She also supports the reading of nonscriptural texts that give inspiration (ibid., 136). But Teresa does not explicitly lay out a method for recollective reading of a text. We can, however, assume that she utilized the method of recollection that was a mainstay of monastic life for centuries, broadly described as *Lectio Divina* (Morello, 1995). The Latin phrase, *Lectio Divina*, literally means, "study of the divine word," or study of Scripture. However, it came to have a very particular method, the one mentioned early in this chapter as the Benedictine form of meditative prayer.

Lectio Divina has a fourfold method which involves *reading a text, meditating on the text, praying over one's concerns*, and *contemplation*. As we approach a text in this method, our primary intent is not intellectual curiosity or argumentation, but seeking an intimate relationship with God. Thus, when we begin reading, we look for a phrase or a few words that provide inspiration in the present moment. That is the reading portion of the method. Then we begin to meditate on those words. We create a short phrase out of the text and ponder it deeply, looking beyond the words for the relationship with God that is evoked. In light of the new insights generated by the meditation, we then enter the arena of prayer and begin to think over our current life concerns. Here we give attention to our life problems or celebrations, bringing them before the inspiration of the text for reflection.

The prayer portion of the experience can evoke emotional responses in us. Sometimes, when we have really prayed through to resolution, there comes a moment of deep peace. This is called contemplation in the fourfold model of prayer.

This contemplation is the same as Teresa's prayer of quiet. When this peace occurs, we are invited to surrender into it. Morello (1995) gives attention to this method of scriptural meditation within Carmelite tradition. It is described in detail in my book, *Christian Meditation and Inner Healing* (1991).

This method is very popular in the West, although we may know it more directly as the method of the "Thought for the Day" in devotional guides or in *A Course in Miracles* (1975). Teresa suggests reading "vernacular" books for inspiration, particularly if we have been away from recollective prayer for some time. She advocates beginning where we are and reading inspiring material with an attitude of recollection.

As you prepare yourself for this experience, find a comfortable chair for sitting with back straight, or you may sit on the floor, with a cushion sufficiently high to allow your back to be straight and your legs relaxed. Bring a writing that you find inspiring. You may wish to explore the Gospels with fresh eyes. If so, my personal recommendation is the Gospel of John, because it contains such rich symbolic imagery. An excellent text with which to begin learning this method is John 15, with its many powerful phrases: "I am the vine, and you the branches"; "I have spoken thus to you, so that my joy may be in you, and your joy complete." Or you may choose just one phrase of the Lord's Prayer, such as "Give us today our daily bread" or "Thy kingdom come, thy will be done, on earth as in heaven" (Matt. 6:9-13). The psalms are another rich source of such phrases, such as "The LORD is my shepherd; I shall want nothing" (Ps. 23). Or you may have a phrase that you regularly use for inspiration, or a favorite book or devotional guide.

Once you have your place and your own position arranged, practice the principle of recollection by simply turning your attention inward. Be aware of your breathing within your chest and abdomen. Spend a few moments being aware of the rising and falling of your body with your breathing. When you notice that your mind is wandering, gently bring it back to the awareness of your breathing. Then take up the phrase you have chosen. Spend a few minutes with it inwardly, repeating it gently to yourself, noticing whether the words are arranged exactly to suit you. It may be that you will want to personalize the phrase somewhat, for example taking the Lord's Prayer phrase, "thy kingdom come, thy will be done, on earth as in heaven," into "thy kingdom come, thy will be done in me today." Take some liberty with adjusting the phrase until it meets your present needs well. Here, we also use Teresa's attention to emotional awareness. Adapt the words until you are comfortable with them. You may notice a rhythm of the words, meeting with your breathing pattern. Then begin to use the phrase inwardly, repeating it and allowing it to bring you into closer relationship with your divine Center.

As you use this prayer of recollection, do not try to suppress your wandering mind. However, if you notice that you have wandered very far from the meaning of the phrase, gently bring your attention back. Much inner teaching is facilitated with this method. Sometimes our inward response to the phrase is uppermost in our awareness, sometimes a life circumstance or memory becomes uppermost, and sometimes the phrase itself is most noticeable. For some people, this method tends to bring more of a mental reflection than a feeling awareness. If this happens, ask yourself to be open to your feelings, and usually you will have more emotional response. Remember that Teresa's imagery places the divine presence at the heart. So it also can be useful to continue the awareness of breathing focused in the trunk of the body, as a way of keeping our attention present to all the dimensions of ourselves, physical and emotional, as well as mental.

As you practice this recollection on a phrase, be aware of the invitation to let it guide you into relationship with God. As that begins to happen, let your phrase change. Often it becomes very simple. It was through this method that the term *Thou* emerged for me many years ago as a primary form of meditative prayer. Let your mind and heart become simple. Notice subtle shifts in breathing and energy that tend to quiet your mind and emotions. Be alert to the interior summons of God to speak your mind and heart simply, laying out your concerns, but also being available for new understandings to emerge.

If moments of peace come, surrender to them. If moments of contemplation come, when you experience divine grace or love, receive them.

RECOLLECTION WITH IMAGINATION ON SCRIPTURE

It is clear from her writings that a primary method of recollective prayer for Teresa was the visual imagination of Scripture stories. For Teresa, this imaginative use of Scripture was especially directed toward her relationship with Christ. In her *Life*, she writes of a time when she was greatly distressed and found comfort in imagining Christ in times of similar distress: "I strove to picture Christ within me, and it did me greater good —in my opinion— to picture Him in those scenes where I saw Him more alone. It seemed to me that being alone and afflicted, as a person in need, He had to accept me" (Kavanaugh and Rodriguez, 1976, 71). In *The Way of Perfection*, she elaborates on her method of choosing a Scripture scene that mirrors her present emotional situation:

> If you are joyful, look at Him as risen. Just imagining how He rose from the tomb will bring you joy. The brilliance! The beauty! The majesty! How victorious! How joyful! Indeed, like one coming forth from a battle where he has gained a great kingdom! And all of that, plus Himself, He desires for you. . . . If you are experiencing trials or are sad, behold Him on the way to the garden: what great affliction He bore in His soul; for having become suffering itself, He tells us about it and complains of it. . . . Or behold Him burdened with the cross, for they didn't even

let Him take a breath. He will look at you with those eyes so beautiful and compassionate, filled with tears; He will forget His sorrows so as to console you in yours, merely because you yourselves go to Him to be consoled, and you turn your head to look at Him. (Kavanaugh and Rodriguez, 1980, 134-35)

This method of meditative prayer, entering into the stories of Scripture with imagination, has been highly identified with the *Spirital Exercises of St. Ignatius* (Mottola, 1964). As you will recall, Ignatius was a contemporary of Teresa. From Teresa's writings, we observe that this method was practiced widely during that time and was not a discovery of Ignatius. His guidebook is for spiritual directors and retreat leaders. It lifts out many themes to be approached through this style of meditative prayer and is a masterful description of the method.

Some people may be attuned to using this method of imaginative prayer with the various scenes of Christ's life. For others, it may seem somewhat artificial or out of keeping with your own inner spiritual resources. One of the most effective ways I have found for approaching this style of meditation in our time is not through the direct scenes of Christ's life, such as those Teresa describes, but instead through the use of imagination in Christ's encounters with people in the Gospels. In guidance on this method, I will use one of those stories. We will work with the story of Jesus stilling the storm (Mark 4:35-41) as a way to approach the possibility of the inner Christ stilling our life's anxiety. Other very powerful stories for this method are the man lame for thirty-eight years (John 5:1-16), the hemorrhaging woman (Mark 5:25-34), and the man born blind (John 9:1-12).

As you prepare yourself for this experience, find a comfortable chair for sitting with back straight, or sit on the floor, with a cushion sufficiently high to allow your back to be straight and your legs relaxed. You could use a Bible, opened to a particular story to which you relate. In this case, I will write out the Scripture story, so that you may use this text directly. Then I will give guidance for accessing this type of imaginative experience.

That day, in the evening, he said to them, "Let us cross over to the other side of the lake." So they left the crowd and took him with them in the boat where he had been sitting; and there were other boats accompanying him. A heavy squall came on and the waves broke over the boat until it was all but swamped. Now he was in the stern asleep on a cushion; they roused him and said, "Master, we are sinking! Do you not care?" He awoke, rebuked the wind, and said to the sea, "Hush! Be still!" The wind dropped and there was a dead calm. He said to them, "Why are you such cowards? Have you no faith even now?" They were awestruck and said to one another, "Who can this be? Even the wind and the sea obey him." (Mark 4:35-41)

Once you have your place and your own position arranged, practice the principle of recollection by turning your attention inward. Be aware of your breathing within your chest and abdomen. Spend a few moments being aware of the rising and falling of your body with your breathing. When you notice that your mind is wandering, gently bring it back to the awareness of your breathing. Turn your attention to the Scripture story.

Begin by imagining the scene of the boat by the shore. Take some time to fill in the details. The more of the inner senses you access, the more vivid your experience will be. Do not be discouraged if you do not have strong visual images. Some people seem to have vivid imagery; others do not, but even so, by working with this method, they receive intriguing insights.

As you imagine the scene by the shore, ask yourself to think of the colors of the sky near dusk. Listen for the sound of the water on the shore line. Is the beach sandy or rocky? What is the temperature? Let your imagination give you your own picture of these circumstances. . . . Notice the two small boats described in the story ready to receive passengers. Then notice the people approaching the boats.

Let your imagination give you your own picture of Jesus
as he might have looked. See the others traveling with
him. Let them embark on the boats in your imagination.
. . . Notice that you now enter the story also and find a
place on the boat in which Jesus is riding. As the boats cast
off, let the sky darken. Night sets in. . . . After a while, you
and the others on the boat make beds for the night on the
deck. Jesus finds a place and is asleep at the rear of the
boat. You fall asleep. . . . Suddenly you are awakened by
violent tossing of the boat. Waves crashing into the boat!
You experience terror and the terror of others, and you
wonder if you will survive. (Now bring your current life
worries and anxieties into the story with you. What fears
are you dealing with? Let yourself experience your fears
and name them. Let your current life issues now enter into
a dialogue with the images of the story.) You and others
notice that Jesus is asleep in the rear of the boat, unaffected
by the storm. Someone yells for him to wake up. Notice
that he then gets up and says to the storm: "Hush! Be still!"

Here I leave my guidance for you to take your own
prayer forward. Hear Jesus' words in the story as your inner meditation phrase: "Hush! Be still!" Hear him saying
those words to your current fears and anxieties. This is a
powerful way to cultivate the strength of the inner Christ.
Can you let your inner Christ arise to greater power than
your anxieties and fears? "Hush! Be still!" Can you let
yourself receive insights and creative solutions to the problems that are creating the anxieties and fears?

Adapt the words until you are comfortable with them.
You also may notice a rhythm of the words aligning with
your breathing pattern. Then begin to use the phrase inwardly, repeating it and allowing it to bring you into
closer relationship with your divine Center. Remember
that Teresa's imagery places the divine presence at the
heart. So it can be useful to continue our awareness of
breathing focused in the trunk of the body, as a way of

keeping our attention present to all the dimensions of ourselves, physical and emotional, as well as mental.

As you practice this recollection on a phrase, be aware of the invitation to let it guide you into relationship with God. If moments of peace come, surrender to them. If moments of contemplation come, when you experience divine grace or love, receive them. This particular imagery can be very effective for guiding us toward the prayer of quiet. As the interior Christ invites us to be still, we may find that we actually are becoming more calm and more attuned with the divine Center within. If this gift of tranquillity comes, receive it gladly.

PRAYER OF RECOLLECTION ON NATURE

In *Interior Castle*, when Teresa introduces the image of the silkworm turning into a butterfly as a metaphor for our spiritual growth, she writes:

> This is enough, Sisters, for a period of meditation even though I may say no more to you; in it you can consider the wonders and the wisdom of our God. Well now, what would happen if we knew the property of every created thing. It is very beneficial for us to busy ourselves thinking of these grandeurs and delighting in being brides of a King so wise and powerful. (Kavanaugh and Rodriguez, 1980, 342)

Teresa describes our observation of nature as a vehicle for our recollection. Imagine the wondrous powers of God, whose ways in nature include the transformation of a silkworm into a butterfly! Though Teresa does not develop a specific prayer of recollection style on nature, I think it is very instructive for us that she includes this description in her writing.

Meditating on the powers of nature, I find, is a marvelous balance to the more inward forms of recollection we have been describing. To enter into the meditative spirit while walking in nature, observing the mysteries of the creation, is to enter the

103

ecstasy of the Holy One, who gives life and sustains life in a billion ways and more on the face of the earth. It is important to notice that Teresa's most graphic metaphors for the spiritual marriage between the individual and God are images of nature: water, fire, butterflies. One kind of union is like two candles whose flames join, but can then be separated again. Another kind of union is like rain falling into a stream; the two cannot be separated. Imagine life as a butterfly, when your life before has been as a worm. In these few words, Teresa invites us into our life as creatures of wonder, in a creation of wonder. June Singer, a Jungian analyst, has published *Seeing Through the Visible World* (1990). The title speaks to the method of recollection that Teresa invites when we gaze upon nature. Teresa suggests that by observing nature, we can open ourselves to communion with the Creator. Here, as in her other forms of recollection, it is useful to remember the centrality of relationship between the individual and God. Cultivation of that relationship is the critical matter, and nature is yet one more vehicle for our learning about God and how to commune with God.

For this experience of recollection, take a walk in a park or another place where you can be close to nature. If large expanses of nature are not available, simply observe an arrangement of flowers. Be aware of your environment. Be aware of the gifts of nature that support and sustain, and indeed create our life. Observe the mysteries of the earth in very specific ways: a ray of sunlight that creates the play of light and shadow on a tree, the color green in all its manifestations, the interplay of bees and flowers, the sweet songs of birds. Notice the cycles of change in nature. Let your own cycles of growth and change be reflected against the cycles of nature. I have found it beneficial to focus on the passage of John 15 and the grapevine, as a metaphor for life in transition. Draw a tree or a plant, identifying the branches that are growing and producing, the roots and nourishment for this stage of your life, the areas of new growth and the areas where growth has ceased. Use nature as a metaphor against which you observe your life circumstances.

After you have gazed on nature in this mode of reverence, close your eyes and let yourself appreciate the divine mystery of life on earth, life within your body. Be aware of mystery. Let it be. Let yourself be.

THE PRAYER OF QUIET

As we begin our discussion of the prayer of quiet, it is useful to remember one of Teresa's key metaphors for interior life: "It should be kept in mind here that the fount, the shining sun that is in the center of the soul, does not lose its beauty and splendor; it is always present in the soul, and nothing can take away its loveliness" (Kavanaugh and Rodriguez, 1980, 289).

As Teresa develops her description of the prayer of quiet and its evolution toward the prayer of union, she uses the metaphor of light, reaching out from the deep interior toward all the faculties, as a primary way to describe the approach of God toward the human being. We can recall here the basic diagram used earlier in this chapter, showing the relationship between surface-level awareness and the deep interior awareness of God. The prayer of quiet is described as moments in which this deep awareness of God visits the surface level of our awareness. In the prayer of quiet, the divine "arms of love" reach out toward the human mind. This is one of Teresa's most graphic descriptions of this experience:

> When His Majesty desires the intellect to stop, He occupies it in another way and gives it a light so far above what we can attain that it remains absorbed. . . . Let the soul enjoy [the presence of God] without any endeavors other than some loving words, for even though we may not try in this prayer to go without thinking of anything, I know that often the intellect will be suspended, even though for only a very brief moment. . . . But one should leave the intellect go and surrender oneself into the arms of love, for His Majesty will teach the soul what it must do at that point.

Almost everything lies in finding oneself unworthy of so great a good and in being occupied with giving thanks. (Ibid., 330-31)

In such moments of quiet, God stills the mind. Perhaps you have experienced this during meditation. Perhaps you have experienced it in other circumstances in your life. One of the most graphic silences I have ever experienced was not during meditation, per se, but during a visit to the redwoods of northern California. My wife, Ruth, and I had traveled as far north as it is possible to go in California. We had parked and, for the better part of an hour, walked through one of the great ancient groves of redwood trees. When we returned to our car and began driving, we were simply silent for another hour together. It was as if God had visited and silenced us. We were so awestruck by the majesty of the forest that words could only diminish the experience.

That is the type of experience that Teresa says visits us in deep meditative prayer. God occupies our minds and silences them. The divine presence in our deepest interior reaches out to bring love and blessing to all our faculties: our emotions, imagination, senses, and intellect or reason. In those moments, we taste the "peace that passes understanding" described in scripture. We may experience this sweet silence in many ways, but the essential ingredient is divine presence, love, and peace. It is important to notice that here Teresa is not describing another type of recollective prayer, but a deeper level of interior experience.

We begin our prayer of recollection by engaging our exterior and interior senses, our rational mind, and in some cases our imagination and feelings. All these faculties are available to our human will, and we exercise them to place ourselves in an interior posture of recollection. When we are visited by the contemplative silence that Teresa calls the prayer of quiet, we are invited into a different way of being present to ourselves. Teresa invites us to notice these moments of quiet and surrender to them. It is as if we have spent our whole life longing for such a moment of serenity. When it comes, will we receive it?

Or will we be so busy with our formal prayer practice that we will not be able to notice it? Teresa advises us to learn to surrender into this silence when it visits us. During those times, we stop our formal practice and dwell in love. What may happen then is that we are inwardly moved to offer words of affection to God, but these spring out of the silence spontaneously. Or we may find ourselves simply delighting in the physical sense of divine presence or inner light. However this experience should come, the task of the prayer of quiet is to learn an inward silent surrender. We are invited here to learn more and more to abandon ourselves into God.

Teresa's interior method is, I think, a very direct mirror of the individual human being learning to let go into trust of God. Here in the deepest interior, we learn to let go of the intellect and of memories. We learn by experiencing a nonattachment to our thoughts that God is more than we could imagine and that as human beings, we possess more dignity than we could have imagined. In the deepest silence, God begins to teach us. Our intuitive wisdom awakens. Teresa's admonitions to those in Mansions III, those who have established a disciplined life of prayer and action, are based on this need to find ultimate release—not in anything we can generate from natural human capacities, but in surrender to a living presence of God.

> Without this sense of abandoning our own efforts, we can become so circumspect, everything offends us because we fear everything; so we don't dare go further.... With humility present, this stage is a most excellent one. If humility is lacking, we will remain here our whole life—and with a thousand afflictions and miseries. For since we will not have abandoned ourselves, this state will be very laborious and burdensome. (Kavanaugh and Rodriguez, 1980, 312-13)

This prayer of quiet "is a little spark of the Lord's true love which He begins to enkindle in the soul; and He desires that the soul grow in the understanding of what this love accompanied by delight is" (Kavanaugh and Rodriguez, 1976, 103).

While there are degrees of this quiet and degrees of delight that accompany it, the essential ingredient of this prayer is our capacity for surrender into the silence and our capacity to allow ourselves to be comforted and granted God's favors. We will explore the variations on this interior awareness of quiet in the following chapter on spiritual experiences.

We cannot really start out in Teresa's understanding of prayer to experience quiet. However, we can be alert to its visitation toward us. Two effective methods of the prayer of recollection may prepare us for this experience. One of the most effective methods to draw us toward this experience is the recollection on the interior diamond or crystal. The image of light emanating from its center invites us to release our thinking process for moments at a time and experience the light of Christ suffusing our whole being. A second type of recollection is to work with the image of Jesus in the boat stilling the storm, until we actually experience his words, "Hush! Be still!" taking root within our heart and mind.

It is intriguing to note the geography of the body in Teresa's descriptions. She invites an awakening of the energy of the heart, which then overcomes and calms the mind. This heart-awakening is described as *gusto,* an experience of profound expansion and joy. She invites us into the heart of love.

THE PRAYER OF UNION

The prayer of union continues and deepens the penetration of God into our whole being. Teresa writes that this experience of union usually does not last more than a "half hour" at a time (Kavanaugh and Rodriguez, 1980, 343). It is in the introduction of this experience in *Interior Castle,* Mansions V, that she speaks of the butterfly emerging from its cocoon:

> When the soul is, in this prayer, truly dead to the world, a little white butterfly comes forth. Oh, greatness of God; How trans-formed the soul is when it comes out of this prayer after having been placed within the greatness of God and so closely joined

with Him for a little while—in my opinion the union never lasts
for as much as a half hour. (Ibid.)

In this deepening surrender into silence, the soul is increas-
ingly taught by God. Teresa sometimes calls this prayer of
union rapture. Sometimes she speaks of it as a period of time of
extreme withdrawal from the external world. Because of the
multitude of possible manifestations that occur during this
prayer of union, we will reserve most of its discussion for the
next chapter. Here, however, I will give the general understanding of the dynamics of this type of prayer.

During the prayer of union, the individual is being initiated
into a life with God, a relationship with the inner teacher,
learning discernment of God's most direct messages to us.
Teresa speaks of learning how to listen for these messages and
gives guidance for us in understanding the multitude of internal experiences that can manifest during this silence.

Fundamental to this experience, however, is not any particular type of spiritual experience, but surrender to the God of
compassionate action, which also finally manifests as a surrender to an awakened serenity within ourselves. One of the great
metaphors Teresa uses to describe this deep silence is the building of Solomon's temple. The temple was the first building to
accommodate the Ark of the Covenant, which contained the
tablets of the Ten Commandments. Prior to the building of the
temple, the Ark was moved from place to place, as the central
mystery of a nomadic people. In the history of Israel, it was the
building of the temple that also marked the establishment of the
kingdom of Israel as an enduring political state. King David had
established this rule; his son Solomon solidified the kingdom
and built the temple. Out of reverence, the temple was so
constructed that all the pieces could be laid in place in total
silence. Imagine the building of a great and beautiful building
with no sound. That is the reference Teresa uses to speak of the
building of the interior temple within the human soul:

109

Every way in which the Lord helps the soul here, and all He teaches it, takes place with such quiet and so noiselessly that, seemingly to me, the work resembles the building of Solomon's temple where no sound was heard. So in this temple of God, in this His dwelling place, He alone and the soul rejoice together in the deepest silence. (Ibid., 441-42)

Thus the prayer of union brings us into the practice of the deepest level of surrender possible, a surrender in which our very personality can be restructured. To understand the depth of this restructuring, it is helpful to observe our diagram of the human being again. (See chart 2.)

Who am I, if I surrender my thinking, my imagination, my emotional responses? Who am I, if I give up my cherished internal memories and my constant self-talk? For Teresa, through the internal reorganization of our soul and mind that comes during the times of deep union, we are finally led toward a true peace with life, with ourselves, and with God.

[The soul] here has no more fear of death than it would of a gentle rapture. . . . There is great detachment from everything and a desire to be always either alone or occupied in something that will benefit some soul. There are no interior trials or feelings of dryness, but the soul lives with a remembrance and tender love of our Lord. It would never want to go without praising Him. (Ibid., 440)

As we reflect on the diagram with which we have been working, suppose we learn to let go of everything less than the divine presence within us? That is what the prayer of union teaches us. Finally, only God is left, renewing our being constantly and guiding us toward daily acts of love in our world. Even the drama of raptures and other inner spiritual experiences cease, until we truly dwell, moment to moment, in the praise and presence of God.

Even as I write, I tremble a bit to ponder this. Certainly, I do not know more in my own existence than moments of quiet,

CHART 2

EXTERIOR WORLD

Mansions I   -

INTERIOR WORLD

SURFACE LEVEL AWARENESS:

Mansions II   *Sensory awareness / Discursive thinking /*
                 Ordinary mental process

Mansions III   - - - - - - - - - - - - - - - - - - - - - - - - - -

Mansions IV   SYMBOLIC LEVEL AWARENESS:

Mansions V   *Imagination/Imagery as tool to deeper quiet/*
                 Emotional awareness

Mansions VI   -

ULTIMATE AWARENESS:

God "enthroned on the heart" /Divine "arms of love"
Experiences of being taught by God in deep silence

both inwardly and outwardly. And that is enough for me at this time of my life. But Teresa invites us into the fullness of the Gospel promise, the reign of God is present and fully available now! And she offers a method of interior awareness that guides us toward this full surrender to God. She knows that this is an awesome promise to receive.

As we go further now in exploring her great catalogue of interior experiences accompanied with this awakening of God, it is important to recognize the place of profound simplicity, inwardly and outwardly, to which she aims our spiritual growth: "This is what I want us to strive for, my Sisters; and let us desire and be occupied in prayer not for the sake of our enjoyment but so as to have this strength to serve" (ibid., 448).

Thus, as in the prayer of quiet, there is really no method to learn here. Rather, there is an inward sensitivity to be cultivated. As we learn to listen for the moments of quiet, we also learn a type of inner surrender, a letting go of attachment to our thoughts. It is not that our thoughts cease, but we learn not to be set off following them. Instead, God occupies our mind and, in silence, begins to teach us in a new way. Our task here, as in learning of the prayer of quiet, is to surrender into these times of deep interior silence. When they come, we learn to invite them into our awareness. Teresa gives us a very important piece of advice—that these experiences of union usually last only for half an hour. If we find ourselves absorbed consistently for longer periods of time, we probably should focus our attention outwardly again. It is important to keep our interior awareness and our exterior life in balance.

And we have the abiding marker from Teresa: Is this practice guiding us toward deeper love of God, self, and others?

Exercises for Reflection and Prayer

1. Keeping a Prayer Journal

One of the most effective ways to deepen your prayer life is to keep a journal of your meditative prayer experience. This assists you in that dual practice of prayer and self-reflection so highly recommended by Teresa. In keeping a prayer journal, you will simply note the date and the form of meditative prayer you have utilized. In regard to the types of prayer we have been discussing, that could be "Meditation on John 15:5," for example; or "Meditation on the Interior Castle"; or "Meditation on Christ." You would then record some of your interior experience.

Often, when people begin a practice of meditative prayer, they find that the first few experiences are not very satisfactory. They may find their minds racing or focusing on very unimportant things. There is a "discipline" and quieting of the mind that will happen over time, when we practice this kind of prayer on a regular basis. Thus the prayer journal is a wonderful way to witness progress over time. Usually, if you will start a practice of meditative prayer for 10 to 30 minutes a day, about 5 times a week, you will witness a marked change in the quality of your inner experience after a month or less. You will begin to be "taught inwardly by God." On average, it has been my experience that 20 minutes is a "natural" period for this kind of reflection.

2. Meditating with a Group

All the meditations described in this chapter can be done with a group. I have given instructions so that they actually can be read out loud by a group leader. If you utilize the meditations in this way, go slowly in your guidance. The mind needs time to hear and respond. Inasmuch as possible, the group leader also should be in an attitude of prayer. By engaging in this attitude, you will find that the reading of the verbal instructions

113

takes on its own slower pace. If you are the leader and enter the attitude of prayer, do pay attention to the volume of your voice. Often there is a tendency for the leader's voice to soften too much to be heard well within the room.

3. Disciplining the Mind

I have given much instruction here in this chapter, with many different forms of meditation. It is most useful to choose ONE form and stay with it for a month or so, particularly at the beginning. This does not mean that you need to stay with one scripture verse, if you are working with Scripture, or that you will have only one prayer phrase, if you are meditating on your relationship with God. These details can change. However, it does seem to assist us in quieting our minds if we utilize only one form of meditative prayer over a period of time. If you are drawn to exactly the same words or image, by all means utilize that form.

4. Bringing Our Whole Selves to God in Prayer

Prayer is most effective when we bring our whole selves, as well as all our concerns to prayer. Thus, include awareness of your feelings, of your body, and of your social and family concerns in your time of prayer. Often people discover an inner rhythm that alternates between the receptive forms of meditative prayer and the more active forms of intercession. By all means, honor the call to intercession when it comes in your prayer time. In many cases, we have a very well-honed practice of intercessory prayer. Those of you who have utilized intercessory prayer effectively may find it most useful to begin your prayer time with intercession, and then shift into the more receptive forms of the prayer of recollection. You will find your own inner rhythm under the guidance of the Holy Spirit. Sometimes meditating on a Scripture phrase becomes "dry." We may seem to be doing only a mental exercise. If you notice something like that happening, then inwardly ask yourself to engage your "feelings" also. You may suddenly find that a whole new world opens up. Or put your awareness into your physical sensations.

Or use the phrase in the context of a prayer for the world. There are many Mansions within each of us, many, many "rooms" to be explored. It is in the spirit of Teresian prayer to bring our whole selves and our whole world before God for blessing, healing, and insight.

5. Integrating the Practice of the Prayer of Recollection with Daily Devotions

If you have a regular practice of daily devotions with *The Upper Room* or other devotional guide, you may find a very natural way to begin practice of the prayer of recollection. Ponder the Scripture verse or "thought for the day" in a prayerful way. That is the spirit of the prayer of recollection on a Scripture phrase. Then write your prayer thoughts in a prayer journal. You will find such a spiritual discipline rather easy to establish when coupled with a daily devotion.

6. Prayer with Collage Images

Teresa invites us into the world of imagination. A very easy way to access our own love of images is to engage in prayer with collage artwork. You will need a blank paper backing of art paper or lightweight cardboard. You also will need a glue stick, scissors, and magazines with a variety of photographs. Background inspirational music can be useful. Look for images that both attract and repel you, those to which you have some emotional reaction. Clip images at will until you seem to have "enough." Then begin to assemble the images, letting the pattern emerge. You can utilize a full-page picture or cut out one image: trees, animals, people. As you assemble the collage, it will begin to tell its own story about your current spiritual concerns. Such a picture then itself sometimes becomes an image for further prayer and reflection. You also can assemble such pictures into a collage journal, noticing themes and images that emerge over several collages. You may discover an image that emerges for yourself that is as powerful for your prayer as Teresa's image of the Interior Castle was for her.

CHAPTER FOUR

Discernment in the Interior World

Happy the enamored heart,
Thought centered on God alone,
Renouncing every creature for Him,
Finding in Him glory and contentment.
Living forgetful of self,
In God is all its intention,
Happy and so joyfully it journeys
Through waves of this stormy sea.

"Happy the Enamored Heart" (Vol. 3, 381),
The Collected Works of St. Teresa of Avila

PRAYER AND IMAGE

 n this chapter we will look more directly at Teresa's experience of the interior world. She was a mistress of deep contemplative prayer. She has described an intriguing array of interior experiences. Her descriptions, together with her understanding, provide invaluable guidance for us in understanding our own experiences of deep prayer.

As we examine these descriptions, we will find that Teresa emphasizes the primacy of discernment in the interior world. In Mansions VI of the *Interior Castle*, she devotes herself to the formidable task of making sense of a whole array of intrapsychic experiences. The importance of this task for Teresa can be

116

seen in the sheer preponderance of material she describes. The total length of *Interior Castle* in the translation by Kavanaugh and Rodriguez is 171 pages. Mansions VI occupies 70 pages of that 171 pages. Clearly, the task of making sense of intrapsychic experience was very important to Teresa. She places a discussion of the discernment of God's will through internal spiritual experiences at the very beginning of Mansions VI.

The emphasis given both to inner life experience and to the task of interior discernment is rooted in the emotional tendencies of her personality. Teresa, as we have previously noted, is much given to highly charged inner visions and voices. Evelyn Underhill, in her writing, *Mysticism*, distinguishes between two great types of spiritual seekers—those who find God primarily as Imminent and those who find God primarily as Transcendent. Underhill's typology in this regard seems to ring true for Teresa, and for her colleague John of the Cross. Teresa discovers the Imminent God within herself through inner visions and voices, with much emotional and devotional content. This is a pathway for the person given to emotion, who often experiences God as Light and as Lover. This type of spirituality is accompanied by much interior activity. Clearly, this was Teresa's way. The other way, the way of finding God primarily as Transcendent, as totally Holy Other, described by Underhill as beyond the capacities of the human mind to grasp through any image, is the path taken by a more intellectual type of personality. Experiences in that pathway are often of God, not as supreme Intimate, but as wholly Awesome, incomprehensible Other, Darkness, the Void. John of the Cross describes this approach to God through the *via negativa*, finding God in emptiness and in the absence of any form—even the form given by the mind in the deepest interior experience.

Both of these two pathways have been given honor and prominence in Christian contemplative writings. The way of Teresa is the way to God by utilizing emotion, inner guidance, interior voices, and visions. It is the way to God embodied in the "flesh" of the interior forms of the psyche. Broadly characterized, it has been called the *kataphatic* way, from the Greek

117

words, *kata*, meaning "with," and *phatic*, meaning "image." It is the way through form. The way of Transcendence, the way of reaching for God beyond the forms of creation, even those most subtle forms of the human mind, is the way called *apophatic*, derived from the terms *apo*, meaning "without," and *phatic*, meaning "image." Inherent in the Christian doctrine of the Incarnation lies the necessity for giving honor to both ways. The Incarnation means that God, the indomitably creative Force beyond any form, whether of flesh or idea, is also fully present in and through form. God becomes fully human in Jesus. Thus, God is accessible both through all forms and beyond all forms.

Other religious traditions sometimes make a hierarchy of these two ways, stating that the apophatic is closer to ultimate perception than the kataphatic. However, it seems to me that Underhill's model is more appropriate for Christian spirituality; she gives equal prominence to these two pathways as appealing to very different personality styles. Teresa is a great guide through the realms of imagination within the human psyche, toward the full embrace of God.

If we recall the model of consciousness with which we have been working, Teresa describes a passage toward God for those who are especially sensitive to the symbolic level of awareness. For these individuals, there is a great deal of interior imagination. The Transcendent type of spiritual seeker may experience very little of this type of interior activity. Teresa validates those individuals who possess a very active interior imagination. I have found it quite useful to recommend the reading of Mansions VI to individuals for whom there is an awakening of interior imaginal experience. They have found it especially helpful to realize that their experiences are not so different from Teresa's, as well as to find that one of the saints of the church described this kind of experience with such clarity.

The distinction between the apophatic and kataphatic way may be seen with these additions to the model of consciousness with which we have been working. (See chart 3.)

CHART 3

EXTERIOR WORLD

Mansion I   -

INTERIOR WORLD

SURFACE LEVEL AWARENESS:

Mansion II   *Sensory awareness / Discursive thinking /*
                      Ordinary mental process

Mansion III   -

Mansion IV   SYMBOLIC LEVEL AWARENESS:

Mansion V   *Imagination / Imagery as tool to deeper quiet /*
                     Emotional awareness

Realm of kataphatic prayer as gateway to ultimate awareness

*Kataphatic prayer receives guidance from this
realm through interior visions and voices.*

Apophatic prayer does not assign meaning to this arena.

Mansion VI   -

Mansion VII   ULTIMATE AWARENESS:

*God "enthroned on the heart" / Divine "arms of love"
Experiences of being taught by God in deep silence*

*Kataphatic prayer brings very deep and subtle
revelations at this level.
Realm of ultimate awareness also accessible
through apophatic prayer.
Revelations for both types beyond words or visions.*

119

TERESIAN DISCERNMENT

Teresa's discussion of discernment offers sound guidance for those experiencing active interior visions and voices. It is critically important that those prone to strong interior imagination have some guidelines for understanding their experiences. Teresa, as a seasoned spiritual guide, is well aware of the potential difficulties of making sense of material that arises from the symbolic level of awareness.

In Mansions VI, she discusses discernment with respect to "locutions," or inner voices. The same type of discussion might take place with other forms of interior experience, such as visions. She begins this discussion by saying that if one hears voices as if from outside oneself, meditative prayer should not be practiced, and the person should engage in exterior activities, such as cleaning house and other physical actions, to balance oneself. We must remember that her advice came long before clinical psychology had enumerated potential psychoses and affective disorders such as depression. However, she demonstrates an acute sensitivity to such problems, discussing the difficulties of the melancholy-prone individual who also hears exterior voices (Kavanaugh and Rodriguez, 1980, 371).

In our time, this suggests a clinically depressed person with schizoid tendencies. Teresa says that this person should not be allowed times of isolation with meditative prayer, as such activity likely will increase the problem: "It is true that it's necessary to be firm in taking prayer away from her and to insist strongly that she pay no attention to locutions" (ibid.). Teresa was thus acutely aware that these interior voices and visions, in and of themselves, do not necessarily lead to health, but must be held in the overall context of what we would call the psychological health of the individual. With that strong warning about potential difficulties, she turns to her discussion for discerning which voices are truly from God.

First of all, she states that it is important not to assume that these voices make one more holy than others: "All good," she says, comes not from hearing voices, but "from how one benefits by these words." As a general guide, she writes, "Pay no more attention to those that are not in close conformity with Scripture than you would to those heard from the devil himself." Finally, she also suggests that if the words come from our own "weak imagination," they should be ignored. We will find that "they will then go away for they will have little effect on you" (ibid., 372). Thus, we begin this process immersed in the wisdom of Scripture, with an understanding of the call to love, personal transformation, and service proclaimed by Christ. With this foundation, we will see clearly that much of our interior imagining is at a very surface level, and we will have a built-in form of inner discrimination to test the messages we receive. Also, her very pragmatic personality points out that those messages that are truly trustworthy will pass the test of time. They will remain of significance to us, while other less important or trustworthy messages will fade from our attention.

Now, having said all these cautionary things, Teresa turns to the positive signs for discerning whether the voices are from God. In this respect, she says, the signs are the same, whether the voices seem to come from an external source or from our interior. In describing these types of experiences, I have sometimes encountered people who have had experiences in which they did hear an exterior voice that they took to be God or Christ, or they had visually seen Christ, or they were physically surrounded by an ecstatic presence that they knew was Christ. For them, even though these forms came in seemingly exterior modes through the senses, they brought forth all the effective changes that Teresa describes as belonging to genuine messages from God. For them, these experiences were life-changing. They were not at all pathological, although the intensity of their divine encounter may have created a rather great dislocation between their ideas about God and their new conviction of God's reality. Teresa's explanation of authentic encounters with God show a very similar and consistent pattern.

Teresa gives three tests as the "surest signs" that voices are from God:

121

1. First, they actually bear authority and power: "[L]ocutions from God effect what they say" (ibid., 372). She illustrates what she means by describing a person in great internal tribulation, to whom the inner voice comes, saying, "Do not be distressed," and the individual is released from the inner disturbance. The message brings about the inner calm that it describes.

2. Second, she says that there is a great "quiet left in the soul," a sense of profound resolution and peace.

3. Third, some of the words "remain in the memory for a very long time, and some are never forgotten" (ibid., 371-73).

These three attributes she further describes as certitude, peace, and interior delight (ibid., 374). Messages from our own imagination do not bear these attributes. In other words, our own imagination may indeed convey divine wisdom to us, but it is without the certitude, peace, and interior delight of the clear encounter with God.

Teresa discusses a variation on these forms of communication with God, as "another way in which the Lord speaks to the soul," and this is called an intellectual vision. This term was in wide use in Teresa's time to describe an inner vision with a clear meaning, which comes suddenly and bears absolute conviction. Her own deepest vision experiences, such as those of her marriage to Christ or her vision of union with God through the Holy Trinity, were such intellectual visions. These are the characteristics of the intellectual vision:

1. First, there is great clarity of the voice. "It is so clear that the soul remembers every syllable and whether it is said in one style or another, even if it is a whole sentence."

2. Second, this insight comes when one is often thinking about something else, or it offers a perspective on the future beyond what one has been consciously thinking or planning. Thus the human imagination cannot have thought of it before.

3. Third, this message comes to one who is in a state of complete receptivity. It is not as if we are actively trying to solve a problem.

4. Fourth, the words themselves seem different from our own use of words and bring with them a sense of their meaning.

5. Fifth, much is simultaneously understood with the words. Much more insight or wisdom is given than we could have imagined.

6. Finally, the message does not lead to inflation but to humility, as the soul is left with great appreciation and gratitude (ibid., 376-77).

Teresa describes what we might call the intuitive mind. Her great contribution is placing these experiences in a theological context, distinguishing the great moments of clarity, insight, and interior guidance from our own surface-level imaginations. Inherent in her model for discernment is a discriminating mind. We are invited by her description into as much self-knowledge as we can gain self-knowledge of our own interior ways of perception and imagination. And we are encouraged to let the divine wholeness that is God guide us in our decisions, in our struggles, and in our visions for the future. Teresa's description is very compatible with an understanding of God as being within each person, and yet also beyond each person. This God is the dynamic, creative, and energizing Force of the universe, and also the One binding all things together in love. In those great moments of sublime vision or interior teaching, this One breaks through in clear and discernible ways to our own minds, giving guidance to us.

This personal guidance from the greatness of God is the true purpose of meditative prayer. Here, we return to Teresa's focus on the alignment of human will with divine will. We find ourselves actually guided toward how we will act in the world, how we will place our life energy in the service of God through these moments of interior knowing. Teresa describes three types of profound discernment experiences: (1) healing, (2) knowledge, and (3) vision for the future. Each of these is essential to our spiritual development. In the first type of locution she describes, we are consciously wrestling with a problem when the voice comes: "Be at peace." It is a breakthrough moment, bringing healing peace. This may come in times of profound distress, as we wrestle over our own personal interior wounds, or over another person's pain in intercessory prayer.

The two types of information Teresa describes as coming during the intellectual vision are of a different nature. One might be described as inner knowledge, a kind of inner teaching, from which we gain much interior insight or understanding about life or human nature, or God, or of the universe. Another type of vision is vision of service. It is an image of the future, to guide our activities and our works of service to the world. Such a vision was Teresa's interior call to build a new type of house of prayer, dedicated to simplicity and contemplative prayer. In all cases, an attitude of deep surrender to the creative energy of God is a prerequisite. We must be earnestly willing to be changed, in order for these divine messages to penetrate us.

Thomas Keating, a present-day Trappist monk, has described the four "consents" that life poses for each of us, from childhood into mature adulthood. The consent of childhood is that of consenting "to the basic goodness of our nature and all its parts" (Keating, 1992, 44). This is the arena in which we may find much childhood wounding that has cut us off from this essential goodness. Here contemplative prayer practice may well focus on the personal emotional healing that we need. The second consent, the consent posed in adolescence, is "to accept the full development of our being by activating our talents and energies" (ibid., 45). Here is the arena in which the interior voice of God may well come as a summons toward a creative future, posing to us the challenge of vision, the challenge of creating new forms for service in the world. The third consent comes in adulthood. It is "to accept the fact of our nonbeing and the diminutions of self that occur through illness, old age, and death" (ibid., 46). In this area, our meditative guidance may lead us to knowledge, understanding, and wisdom regarding the nature of life and the nature of God. We may find solace in living our passing lives under the eternality of God or, in a flash of insight, we may learn to accept life's diminishments, as did Job. Finally, and perhaps most important, Keating states that we must consent "to be transformed" (ibid.). That willingness—in humility, day after day—to allow our very personalities and priorities to be changed is to stand in the creative presence of

God. Teresa assumes our willingness to be changed and our willingness to submit our lives for transformation, when she summons us to a spirituality of the cross, rather than of particular inner experiences.

As Teresa describes her own interior experiences of connection with God, there is a fourth major category. That category is joy, ecstasy, pure praise of God. Thus, the four major types of interior experience Teresa describes when we are deeply touched by God are experiences of: (1) healing, (2) knowledge, (3) vision, and (4) joy.

While we have touched on a myriad of specific interior experiences in our previous discussions regarding the deepening quiet of Teresa's meditative prayer method, the remainder of this chapter will be devoted to restating particular inner experiences in a way that will make them accessible to contemporary practitioners of contemplative prayer. In these discussions, we will utilize the descriptions of inner experiences that pertain to the general categories of healing, knowledge, vision, and joy.

It is important to notice how frequently Teresa speaks of a shift from exterior to interior awareness. In a variety of ways, she describes a fundamental shift of allegiance within our daily life and awareness –away from what we have been calling ordinary awareness, very much influenced by our relationship to the exterior world, by the senses, and by the intellect. Teresa describes an education of our interior modes of perception toward another kind of perception, a perception of what we have been calling ultimate reality. The means of access toward this new type of perception comes through learning the ways of the symbolic realm.

When Teresa invites us into a complete transformation of the personality, practiced in times of deep silence, I think she is inviting us to discern what we might call the "authentic" self within us. This authentic self is rooted in a deep knowledge of God, an intuitive perception of the total needs of our world, and our own capacity to interface with those needs in ways of meaningful service. This alignment of our awareness and self-perception with the deep intuitive voice within ourselves provides the capacity for the divine will to speak directly to us.

DISCOVERING THE "SECRET PLACE" WITHIN

Teresa invites us to discover the "secret place," where exchange between God and the soul can take place (Kavanaugh and Rodriguez, 1980, 284). It takes prayer and self-reflection to discover this interior place, which is different from the senses or other faculties such as emotion and intellect (ibid.). Prayer leads to a "suspension" of the faculties as we learn a direct perception of the love of God. This practice enables us to become servants of love. In the process, we learn no longer to be dominated by the intellect but to use the intellect in the service of love. She admonishes us to move on from our little works. She makes it clear that these are not only "little works" in the world but "little works" in the superficial way we relate to God (Kavanaugh and Rodriguez, 1980, 307). In order to move on, we must learn detachment (ibid., 309-10). Have we been willing to surrender our whole lives, including our own interior way of relating to reality? Teresa asks for nothing less. Love finally must reach the point of overwhelming reason within ourselves (ibid., 312), until we are finally able to abandon ourselves (ibid.) and surrender into the "arms of love" (ibid., 331).

This radical change for Teresa is not unlike what we might call an ego-death, a complete internal change in the way we perceive and relate to reality, and even to our own personal identity. Indeed, we are being changed from the human to the divine Center within. This radical change occurs as we practice the prayer of quiet and the prayer of union. You see, in these experiences, God suspends us from our habitual thought patterns and emotional responses. We close our eyes and suspend ourselves from external sensory awareness. This is the act of weaving the cocoon of transformation around ourselves.

In these times of deep silence, when the faculties and senses are "asleep," God enters our consciousness. We are thus likened

126

in our meditative silence to being dead, awaiting regenerative transformation, like Christ's resurrection. In that silence, a new and fit dwelling place for divine love is being built, like Solomon's temple.

The psychic and physical energy released in such a transformative process is very great. It results in all kinds of unusual experiences, first opening us to receive these "whispers" of love (ibid., 362) from God, then overwhelming us in a process of surrender. And finally, God creates a new equilibrium of selfhood within us, as a vehicle for divine love to be evidenced in the world.

In this description, Teresa validates the experiences of many people in our time. Although these forms of inner experience were considered suspect in Teresa's time, there was widespread practice of illuminative prayer during the sixteenth century. In our time, the interest in esoteric matters, in developing intuitive knowledge of all kinds, was paralleled in Teresa's time by the practice of sustained silence. The church looked with suspicion upon such practices then, particularly among the women known as the *alumbrados*—laywomen practicing sustained prayer on their own—much as our time looks with suspicion upon the various ventures into the inner realms being undertaken by many people on their own. For these reasons, Teresa's catalogue of interior experience can serve a very important validating function for people in our time who may be experiencing such things without benefit of the cloister.

Teresa speaks of many types of particular experience, among them locutions, or interior words that seem to be spoken by God (ibid., 372), interior visions (ibid., 380), such quiet that the body becomes cold and breathing seems almost to cease (ibid., 384), out-of-body experiences (ibid., 388), and perhaps speaking in tongues (ibid., 395). Underlying all these is Teresa's deep and abiding conviction that in these experiences, meaning is being conveyed, often with such power that we cannot fully bring back the experience with our memory.

127

When the soul is in this suspension, the Lord likes to show it some secrets, things about heaven, and imaginative visions. It is able to tell them afterward, for these remain so impressed on the memory that they are never forgotten. But when the visions are intellectual, the soul doesn't know how to speak of them. For there must be some visions during these moments that are so sublime that it's not fitting for those who live on this earth to have the further understanding necessary to explain them. However, when the soul is again in possession of its senses, it can say many things about these intellectual visions. (Ibid., 380)

Teresa likens this experience to Jacob's vision of angels ascending and descending the ladder. "By means of the ladder Jacob must have understood other secrets that he didn't know how to explain, for by seeing just a ladder on which angels descended and ascended, he would not have understood such great mysteries if there had not been deeper interior enlightenment" (ibid.). She also speaks of the empowerment that came to Moses through his vision of the burning bush. "But he must have understood such deep things among the thorns of that bush that the vision gave him courage to do what he did for the people of Israel. So, Sisters, we don't have to look for reasons to understand the hidden things of God" (ibid., 381). These experiences of great illuminative awareness are likened to being shown the treasure room of a very wealthy person. It is so grand that the mind can scarcely comprehend it.

A general term given by Teresa to these experiences is *rapture*. One of the specific types of raptures is a "quick" rapture.

It is such that the spirit truly seems to go forth from the body. On the other hand, it is clear that this person is not dead; at least, he cannot say whether for some moments he was in the body or not. It seems to him that he was entirely in another region different from this in which we live, where there is shown another light so different from earth's light that if he were to spend his whole life trying to imagine that light, along with the other things, he would be unable to do so. It happens that within an instant so many things together are taught him that if he were to work for many years with his imagination and mind in order to systematize them, he wouldn't be able to do so, not even one thousandth part of one of them. (Ibid., 388-89).

This quick rapture brings great wisdom and seems to touch upon realms very different from earthly reality. In such visions, sometimes one sees "saints" and recognizes who they are without being told, or one may see "a multitude of angels with their Lord" (ibid., 389). "Whether all this takes place in the body or not, I wouldn't know; at least I wouldn't swear that the soul is in the body or that the body is without the soul" (ibid.). This experience, she also calls an "interior flight," and states that "though noiseless, [it] is so clearly a movement that it cannot be the work of the imagination" (ibid.).

Such deep and sublime experiences can bring dissatisfaction with worldly life. "From then on life on earth is very painful, and it doesn't see anything good in those things that used to seem good to it. The experience causes it to care little about them" (ibid., 389-90). This type of experience mirrors John of the Cross's description of the dark night of the senses, in which worldly life brings much less satisfaction than before, because such sublime experience of God is being given directly. It is also intriguing to note how parallel such meditative experience is to the "near death" experience so frequently reported in our time. A similar dislocation from ordinary patterns in daily life often accompanies such direct epiphany. A search for meaningful service within the world often results from such direct experience of the "light of God," whether received in meditation or in the near-death experience.

The onset of this type of deep experience may be accompanied by mental confusion: "Well then, if a person in this state who knows how to read well takes up a book in the vernacular, he will find that he understands no more of it than if he didn't know how to read even one of the letters, for the intellect is incapable of understanding" (ibid., 364). In this respect, Teresa mirrors John of the Cross's descriptions of midnight during the dark night of the soul, when the mental processes themselves are undergoing transformation (Kavanaugh and Rodriguez,

1974, 344). John of the Cross's description of this process is very graphic:

> Since this night not only purges the intellect of its light and the will of its affections, but also the memory of its discursive knowledge, it is fitting that the memory be annihilated in all things to fulfill what David said of this purgation: I was annihilated and knew not [Ps. 72:22]. David's unknowing refers to forgetfulness and a lack of knowledge in the memory. This abstraction and oblivion is caused by the interior recollection in which this contemplation absorbs the soul.
>
> That the soul with its faculties be divinely tempered and prepared for the divine union of love, it must first be engulfed in this divine and dark spiritual light of contemplation, and thereby be withdrawn from creature affections and apprehensions. The duration of this absorption is proportionate to the intensity of the contemplation. (Ibid.)

Teresa describes a similar absence of the mind from anything other than God during these raptures: "He doesn't want any hindrance from anyone, neither from the faculties nor from the senses, but He immediately commands the doors of all these dwelling places to be closed; and only that door to His dwelling place remains open so that we can enter" (Kavanaugh and Rodriguez, 1980, 383). However, it is significant to see that for Teresa, the visionary experiences during these raptures are filled with meaning. Thus, the depth of emptiness described by John of the Cross may be somewhat ameliorated in a visionary of Teresa's temperament.

> In a rapture, believe me, God carries off for Himself the entire soul, and, as to someone who is His own and His spouse, He begins showing it some little part of the kingdom that it has gained by being espoused to Him. However small that part of His kingdom may be, everything that there is in this great God is magnificent. (Ibid., 382)

EXPERIENCING HEALING, KNOWLEDGE, VISION, AND JOY

In exploring the ways God speaks directly to us, Teresa described a breadth of modes of contact between God and the individual. Much of Teresa's own meditative experience was the occasion for interior knowledge or joy. Her writings bear no trace of the split between piety and action that influences so much discussion of spirituality in our time. For Teresa, God acts within the individual, uplifting, healing, inspiring, and guiding. All these ways are present to us in times of deep prayer. When we enter into the crucible of prayer, we do not know what God will bring. When we are met by the Divine Embrace, we receive it, with the joy of interior delight or with the agony of transformation. God may speak to us, healing our interior pain or presenting us with a challenge of great action to be brought to completion within the world. We will conclude this chapter with a brief discussion of each of these discrete types of experience.

Healing

We devoted direct attention to the experiences of healing in our discussion of Mansions IV and V, in which Teresa makes the distinction between *gustos* and *contentos* (see chapter 2). *Contentos* are experiences which may be accompanied by deep emotional release, by tears, and by physical pain that is felt and released. These experiences are quite different from *gustos*, experiences of profound joy, accompanied by a sense of divine energy that seems to "open the heart." We also see a type of healing experience when Teresa discusses the breakthrough moments when a locution gives "peace" to us as we pray about a troubling situation. Teresa suffered an enormous amount of physical pain, through which her body engaged in a type of prayer for healing release. The indications are that such release did come.

131

Knowledge

In many cases, she writes of the situation in which we are taught by God in times of deep absorption. Often, for Teresa, this absorption reached a point at which the body was cold, and there seemed to be complete withdrawal from the physical world. Many practitioners of meditative prayer may never reach this state of interior absorption, although they may experience similar flashes of insight while meditating. Teresa's own images of the interior castle or the soul being like a crystal, or of sin being like the crystal covered with pitch, show that these teachings can take the form of image as well as of words. Teresa's own personality tended toward locutions or images in which profound understanding of God or of life were given. Through her writings, we are encouraged to listen for our own modes of receiving interior guidance and give attention to learning in order to understand their messages.

We also can notice how profoundly Teresa's understanding of Scripture was influenced by her interior experience. Because of the vividness of her own interiority, she has great appreciation for God's ability to speak directly to Jacob in his vision of the angels ascending and descending, or to Moses in the burning bush. Similarly, with awakening interior understanding, contemplatives in our time will find Scripture enlivened with a new understanding of the Holy One's capacity to speak Eternal wisdom to people of all times and places. In our age, we have largely lost the sense of reverence and awe that accompanied the great sagas of Scripture. When we touch the Holy Sepulchre within ourselves, we find Scripture again ablaze with God. It is useful to notice how much of Teresa's writings offer wisdom on the nature of life. When Teresa experienced the deprivation of the inspiring books taken away by the Inquisition, she was told, in her interior divine voice, that she herself would become a living book of God.

She encourages us to approach God as the great Teacher, enabling us to live with wisdom, detachment, commitment, and serenity. She invites us to learn wisdom from within and to become living books of God for our time.

Vision

Teresa was sustained by a very particular vision for her active life work. We will speak about it in some detail in the next chapter. That vision was the belief that God asked her to found a new house of prayer, returning to the simplicity of the Carmelite rule. She felt profoundly called to act this vision out in the world. She believed that this was a direct summons from God. Teresa's life invites each of us to search for that divine summons to vision and action for our own lifetime. In this respect, Teresa follows the guidance of the great biblical figures. She awaits a call and responds when that call comes. This particular calling was very difficult for Teresa to bring to fruition. In our time, so enamored with instantaneous results, Teresa stands as an extraordinary model of persistence against great odds to bring her vision into action. Teresa's experience invites us to receive a great calling and to act upon it.

Joy

Finally, Teresa was sustained by divine joy. Her experiences of joy are nowhere better illustrated than in this description:

> In the midst of these experiences that are both painful and delightful together, our Lord sometimes gives the soul feelings of jubilation and a strange prayer it doesn't understand. I am writing about this favor here so that if He grants it to you, you may give Him much praise and know what is taking place. It is, in my opinion, a deep union of the faculties; but our Lord nonetheless leaves them free that they might enjoy this joy—and the same goes for the senses—without understanding what it is they are enjoying or how they are enjoying. What I'm saying seems like gibberish, but certainly the experience takes place in this way, for the joy is so excessive the soul wouldn't want to enjoy it alone but wants to tell everyone about it so that they

might help this soul praise our Lord. All its activity is directed to this praise. Oh, how many festivals and demonstrations the soul would organize, if it could, that all might know its joy! (Ibid., 395)

This language seems to reflect a type of "speaking in tongues," or at least an internal "prayer" language that is accompanied with great joy. The key point is that Teresa relishes experiences of ecstasy, joy, and rapture. She cherishes the presence of God as an experience of great pleasure. She invites us to delight in the Lord.

And what are we to make of her marriage with God? Such a profound completion of her interior longing for a full union with God involves an inner healing of the deepest human split between individual personality and God. It also involves a new and more intimate knowledge of God. For Teresa, it involved a sense of joy, and it gave new meaning and new tasks to her life work. All levels of experience came to joyous fruition in her image of being married to Christ or her vision of union to God through the Holy Trinity.

Thus, the practice of Teresa's interior experiences awaken the individual to a vital divine presence, acting in and through the individual in ways that are very compatible with scripture. Her life and writings on these matters invite our own interior lives to awaken to the possibility of divine presence and guidance.

Exercises for Reflection and Prayer

1. Healing, Knowledge, Vision, Joy

How do you relate to God at this time in your life—is it for healing, for wisdom, for sustaining vision, for joy? Perhaps you are familiar with each of these ways of relating to God. Perhaps there is one that you feel is more dominant than the others. Spend some time with your prayer journal, writing about your relationship to God as Healer, Teacher, Guide, and Joyous companion.

2. How do you decide?

The issue of discernment is a very prominent theme in discussions of spiritual formation. Put simply, discernment is the process whereby we make our daily and major life decisions in companionship with God. Has Teresa's discussion of discernment assisted you in any way to understand your own decision process more clearly? Think about a major life decision you have made in the past. How did you go about gathering information; how did you think and pray about the decision; with whom did you discuss it in order to get information? How did you finally make the decision? Did you feel that God was with you in the decision process? What does it mean to you to ask God into your decision processes?

3. Interior Spiritual Experience

Teresa gives an intriguing catalogue of interior experiences. Some of these may be familiar to you. Some may seem quite foreign. Perhaps you have had one or more "life-changing" spiritual experiences in your life. How are these experiences similar to and different from the kinds of experiences Teresa describes? Perhaps your experiences of God are more outwardly oriented than those of Teresa. Perhaps you find God most fully alive for you in the midst of a work project or in conversations with people, or in a worship service or in relationship to nature. Describe where and how God is most alive for you.

CHAPTER FIVE

Surrender and Action

Teresian Prayer for Contemporary Lives

Give me wealth or want,
Delight or distress,
Happiness or gloominess,
Heaven or hell,
Sweet life, sun unveiled,
To You I give all.
What do You want of me?

Give me, if You will, prayer;
Or let me know dryness,
An abundance of devotion,
Or if not, then barrenness,
In you alone, Sovereign Majesty,
I find my peace,
What do You want of me?

Give me then wisdom.
Or for love, ignorance,
Years of abundance,
Or hunger and famine.
Darkness or sunlight,
Move me here or there:
What do You want of me?

If You want me to rest,
I desire it for love;
If to labor,
I will die working:
Sweet Love say
Where, how and when.
What do You want of me?

Calvary or Tabor give me,
Desert or fruitful land;
As Job in suffering
Or John at Your breast;
Barren or fruited vine,
Whatever be Your will:
What do You want of me? . . .

Yours I am, for You I was born:
What do You want of me?

From "In the Hands of God" (Vol. 3, 378-79),
The Collected Works of St. Teresa of Avila

OBEDIENCE AND LIBERTY OF SPIRIT

 here is no issue more central to Teresa's spirituality than the relationship between obedience and the cultivation of liberty of the spirit. These two positions, seemingly at odds in our time, were cultivated only in mutuality for Teresa. Some of her writings on this theme will seem extremely demanding to contemporary ears. Yet when we look beyond the specific forms of obedience that Teresa championed and examine the tension she felt between obedience to God and obedience to her confessors and superiors, we will

137

discover principles that can be readily applied to the search for contemporary spiritual authenticity.

For Teresa, obedience is the cornerstone of spiritual growth. We recall her focus on the alignment of the human will with the divine will as the organizing principle for personal spiritual growth. This alignment of wills is not to be practiced only in an interior surrender, but also in action in the exterior world. Obedience for Teresa is a spiritual practice that is as important and, ultimately, as fruitful in spiritual development as the practice of interior prayer. As was customary in monastic life, Teresa views obedience as submission to one's personal confessor or superior. As we have noted, often Teresa herself experienced great tension between her own interior urges and the commands and requests of her confessors and superiors. As she began writing *The Foundations* (Kavanaugh and Rodriguez, 1985), however, she seems able to view all the conflicts from a very mature stance. *The Foundations,* yet another book her superiors asked her to write, was begun in 1573, nine years before her death and four years prior to writing *Interior Castle. The Foundations* recounts the numerous trials of founding monasteries throughout Spain, an activity in which Teresa engaged continuously from 1567 until her death in 1582. In fact, her final illness came upon her during the process of founding a house.

By 1573, she was able to observe the remarkable spiritual maturity that accompanied the strenuous practice of obedience over many years. This obedience for Teresa was as apt to be in exterior actions as in matters of interior discernment. She writes:

There was a person to whom I spoke a few days ago who for about fifteen years was kept so busy through obedience with work in occupations and government that in all those years he didn't remember having one day for himself, although he tried the best he could to keep a pure conscience and have some periods each day for prayer. His soul in its inclination is one of the most obedient I have seen, and so he communicates this spirit of obedience to all those with whom he deals. The Lord has repaid him well; for he has found that he has, without knowing how, that same precious and desirable liberty of spirit that the perfect have. In it, they find all the happiness that could be wanted in this life, for in desiring nothing they possess all. Nothing on earth do they fear or desire, neither do trials disturb them, nor do consolations move them. In sum, nothing can take away their peace because these souls depend only on God. . . .

This is not the only person, for I have known others of the same sort, whom I had not seen for some, or many, years. In asking them about how they had spent these years, I learned that the years were all spent in the fulfillment of the duties of obedience and charity. On the other hand, I saw such improvement in spiritual things that I was amazed. Well, come now, my daughters, don't be sad when obedience draws you to involvement in exterior matters. Know that if it is in the kitchen, the Lord walks among the pots and pans helping you both interiorly and exteriorly. (Kavanaugh and Rodriguez, 1985, 119-20)

Teresa provides this illuminating synthesis of her views on obedience:

The highest perfection obviously does not consist in interior delights or in great raptures or in visions or in the spirit of prophecy but in having our will so much in conformity with God's will that there is nothing we know he wills that we do not want with all our desire, and in accepting the bitter as happily as we do the delightful when we know that His majesty desires it. This seems most difficult (not the doing of it, but this being content with what completely contradicts our nature); and indeed it truly is difficult. But love has this strength if it is perfect, for we forget about pleasing ourselves in order to please the one we love. (Ibid., 120)

The practice of obedience has led Teresa and the others whom she admires in these writings to find contentment in trials as well as delights, when the cause is perceived as worthy of obedience.

With these terms before us, however, it is extremely useful to view Teresa's own struggles with external authorities regarding the foundation of her first house under the primitive rule, St. Joseph's of Avila. In 1560, during a major period of visionary experiences culminating in the reception of her wounding in the heart, Teresa also began to believe that she was commanded by God to establish a new form of house of prayer for women.

Thus, the originating vision for the founding of this house came from Teresa's own inner urgings. She wrote at length of the founding of St. Joseph's in *Life* (Kavanaugh and Rodriguez, 1976). She had heard God command her to build a new house, one that would follow the primitive rule of the Carmelites. She wanted a small house, with a small number of women who would practice a simple life. In distinction to the popular and large convents under the mitigated rule, such as the Incarnation with its 150 women, this new house would be fully devoted to the cultivation of interior spirituality, shedding many of the social conventions of the day. She was sufficiently inspired to begin inquiries about founding such a new house, but she was rebuked by her own community of nuns:

> I was very much disliked throughout my monastery because I had wanted to found a more enclosed monastery. They said I was insulting them; that in my own monastery I could also serve God since there were others in it better than I; that I had no love for the house; that it would be better to procure income for this place than for some other. Several of them said I should be thrown into the prison cell; others—very few—defended me somewhat. I saw clearly that in many matters my opponents were right, and sometimes I gave them explanations. Yet since I couldn't mention the main factor, which was that the Lord had commanded me to do this, I didn't know how to act; so I remained silent about the other things. (Ibid., 220)

She had resistance from the town council of Avila, which objected to another religious house, and she could find no benefactor to support it. Then, after working toward the establishment of this house, the Father Provincial changed his mind and rescinded his approval. During this trying time, Teresa yielded to the will of both religious and secular authorities.

She found herself surprisingly content with this decision, but she was greatly distressed that her confessor now seemed to question her divine urging in these matters. For five or six months, she writes, she lived in silence with these concerns. However, her confessor asked her to speak with the Father Rector who came to visit. As she shared in full honesty with him regarding these matters, he confirmed that her vision of the new monastery was of God. With this information, her confessor encouraged her to again seek its founding.

During this time of new energy toward the establishment of the house, she found surprising sources of encouragement. She secretly began plans to create this house, having others buy a house and begin remodeling it. While she was sent to care for a woman who was ill, she met Maria de Jesus, a woman who had walked to Rome and returned with permission to establish an independent house. Maria also informed Teresa of the original charge to the Carmelite houses that they be houses of poverty. Thus Teresa discovered that her own desire for utter simplicity for this new house was in fact confirmed in the founding vision of their order. Inspired by these discoveries, she continued her efforts, seeking an independent letter of foundation from Rome. As preparations proceeded, her uncle inhabited the house being prepared. He became quite ill, and Teresa asked and received permission to stay with him. For several months, she was able to oversee the remodeling while looking after her uncle. Teresa viewed all these circumstances as God blessing her work.

She describes an extraordinary vision that sustained her in this work and encouraged her to work without the consent of all of her superiors:

> I saw our Lady at my right side and my father St. Joseph at the left, for they were putting that robe on me. I was given to understand that I was now cleansed of my sins. After being clothed and while experiencing the most marvelous delight and glory, it seemed to me then that our Lady took me by the hands. She told me I made her very happy in serving the glorious St. Joseph, that I would believe that what I was striving for in regard

141

to the monastery would be accomplished, that the Lord and those two would be greatly served in it, that I shouldn't fear there would ever be any failure in this matter even though the obedience which was to be given was not to my liking, because they would watch over us, and that her Son had already promised us He would be with us, that as a sign that this was true she was giving me a jewel. . . . As for what the Queen of Angels said concerning obedience, it pertained to the fact that it distressed me not to give obedience to the order, but the Lord had told me it wasn't suitable to give it to my superiors. He gave me the reasons why it would in no way be fitting that I do so. But He told me I should petition Rome in a certain way, which He also indicated to me, and that He would take care that we get our request. And so it came about, for the petition was made the way the Lord told me and it was granted easily, whereas we had been unable to obtain it. (Ibid., 226-27)

Here we note the compelling way her prayer inspired, indeed, dictated her actions. Whether in our time, we call this profound intuition or divine inspiration, it is clear that Teresa knew a profoundly inspired source of inner guidance, cultivated through years of meditative prayer. When the time came for great action, this divine Center inspired and guided her.

Finally, all arrangements were ready, and she had Mass celebrated in the new house. This was the first time the public gained any knowledge of what was transpiring. The city council was furious, as were the religious authorities. A lawsuit was brought by the city council against Teresa on August 29, 1562. Finally, Teresa gained the approval from one sympathetic official within the church, and resolution was made with the city. Teresa moved into St. Joseph's with four nuns in December.

This story is worth retelling in some detail, because it sheds such light on Teresa's view of obedience. She yields to external authorities, to be sure. But her highest allegiance is to her perceived divine summons. Over time, this interior vision was tested, and Teresa herself was sorely tested. When she had tried conventional ways to obtain permission, she was blocked at every turn. But what finally emerged is a house with even greater autonomy than she would have been able to envision—the freedom of poverty (thus not looking for a major donor before beginning) and autonomous permission from Rome to establish this house.

Eleven years later, as she began writing *The Foundations*, we discover that she was much surprised when religious authorities asked her to undertake the founding of similar houses. In doing so, she found herself often using the strategies she had learned at St. Joseph's. When asked to create a new house, she and a few nuns would go in secret at night, then work until morning to make a suitable place for Mass. Once Mass was said the next morning, the presence of the house was established, often to the shock of the town. Teresa trusted that benefactors would come forth to support the house afterward, rather than carefully planning such benefaction beforehand.

In *The Foundations*, Teresa tells of her trepidation when the Father General visited Spain from Rome. This type of visit had never before occurred. She feared that he would disapprove of the new foundation of St. Joseph's. Even worse, she feared that he would command her to go back to live at the monastery of the Incarnation, where she would live again in the noisy community of 150 women under the mitigated rule. However, she arranged for him to visit St. Joseph's, and to her surprise, not only was her work at St. Joseph's approved, but the Father General gave her papers for the direct establishment of numerous other houses under the primitive rule. Moreover, he forbade the local provincial religious authorities to interfere with her efforts. In their discussions, they decided that houses for men also should be established. Thus, from a very arduous beginning, Teresa was given autonomous authority to replicate St. Joseph's throughout Spain. Her personal obedience to God now found confirmation in a new challenge of obedience to the church as she began her remarkable activities.

After Teresa had managed to gain favor in the styles of houses she was establishing, in 1571, much to her dismay, she was appointed prioress of the large monastery of the Incarna-

143

tion. This story briefly shows more eloquently than through mere concepts what Teresa meant by obedience. She walked between two centers of authority—the internal divine callings made clear by the practiced prayer of recollection and the external authorities who required particular kinds of public service. Teresa learned that both can be divine voices. In fact, although she went unenthusiastically to the Incarnation, she also managed to reform it over a few years. She brought John of the Cross as the confessor and created a climate for spiritual renewal among the 150 women there, although she did so under their mitigated rule, rather than under the primitive rule. Thus she demonstrated her dedication to purpose and flexibility of methods.

Teresa also utilized "learned men" for advice. She went to more than one source for opinions regarding her inner visions, as well as her exterior work. It would not be unfair to say that Teresa devised a kind of "ad hoc committee" of advisors. Obedience for Teresa occurred within the milieu of the religious community of her time. She did not make unexamined decisions based solely on her interior urgings and visions. She tested them for authenticity of concept with trusted advisors and allowed external circumstances to mold the final outcome.

While it seems fair in analyzing Teresa's life to say that her ultimate obedience was to her interior messages from God, it is equally true that we would have missed some of her most eloquent writings, had she not held herself in obedience to her superiors. Both *Interior Castle* and *The Foundations* were specifically requested by her superiors. These books were not tasks that she relished, yet she performed them because of the requests of others. The same reality is true of many of the houses she established in Spain. The proliferation of these houses was not due so much to Teresa's personal initiative as to her response to requests from superiors that came her way. In fact, in some cases, endowments were offered in communities too small to support a house. Even on a point as important to Teresa as the poverty of houses, she gave way to make exceptions.

TERESIAN DISCERNMENT

What principles for our own discernment of active service can we draw from Teresa's writings and example? In our time, the resurgence of interest in matters of the interior is justly criticized, if such interest does not lead to social health as well as personal health. The danger does not lie in the practice of meditation and prayer, but rather in the lack of social context in which they are practiced. Teresa's reliance upon the guidance of others, even delaying her cause or undertaking new work because of others, meant that she had a constant social web in which her interior callings could be challenged, tested, and ultimately perfected, in a way that would contribute effectively to reorganizing society in her time. For this reason the church usually has held personal prayer and meditation as only one spiritual discipline among many. The other disciplines include worship within a church community, social engagement in acts of charity, sharing wealth, studying scripture and other sources of wisdom, caring for the weak within the church and within one's community.

From the perspective of Teresa, there is danger in the exploration of inner awareness apart from religious tradition or religious community. That danger, quite simply, is that we may fail to hear God's call to sacrificial service. I realize full well that these terms are highly explosive in our time of individual liberation and personal empowerment. Yet collectively, we must acknowledge that we are allowing the fabric of our society to disintegrate with a kind of apathy that is alarming. When local governments no longer can pass school-bond initiatives, when crack babies continue to be born, when ethnic wars threaten the disruption of all civility in parts of the globe, when nations face the possibility of civil war, Teresa would ask all of us, I think, to examine our resistance to the very concept of obedience. In our time, we must find a new way to articulate our understanding of obedience to God as a summons from within our individual hearts toward deeds of service undertaken in compassion for the common good.

145

For Teresa, final liberty came not through blissful states of consciousness, although she cherished these. Final liberty came in yielding one's personal desires to the greater tasks given to her by God and her religious community. She toiled often under duress and found the crucible of that toiling to be the place of greatest spiritual maturing. She would unashamedly invite us to undertake great tasks that stir our hearts, to let them be shaped and given form in the conflict and constructive dialogue with the ideas of others.

Here she shows her understanding of the dynamic that develops between obedience and inner freedom of will:

> By exercising ourselves in this surrender, sometimes denying ourselves, at other times waging a thousand battles since the judgment made in our case seems to us absurd, we come to be conformed with what they command us. It can be a painful exercise, but with or without the pain we in the end do what is commanded, and the Lord helps so much on His part that for the same reason that we subject our will and reason to Him He makes us lord over our will. Then, being lords of ourselves, we can with perfection be occupied with God, giving Him a pure will that He may join it with His, asking Him to send fire from heaven so that His love may burn this sacrifice and take away everything that could displease him. We have done what we can by placing the sacrifice on the altar, although through much hardship. And, insofar as is in our power, the sacrifice remains on the altar and does not touch the ground.
>
> Clearly, no one can give what he does not have; he must have it first. Well, believe me that in order to acquire this treasure there is no better way than to dig and toil in order to excavate from this mine of obedience. The more we dig the more we shall find; and the more we submit to men, having no other will than that of our superiors, the more we shall be lords over our will so as to bring it into conformity with God's will. (Kavanaugh and Rodriguez, 1985, 121-22)

We must notice that this transformation through obedience is honed in a spirit of prayer and petitions for divine help. Prayer ultimately empowers us for service. And the efficacy of our interior visions is tested in active service.

Observe, Sisters, whether leaving the pleasure of solitude is not well repaid. I tell you that it is not because of a lack of solitude that you will fail to dispose yourselves to reach this true union that was mentioned, that is, to make your will one with God's. That is the union that I desire and would want for all of you, and not some absorptions, however delightful they may be, that have been given the name "union." . . . Here, my daughters, is where love will be seen: not hidden in corners but in the midst of the occasions of falling. . . . As for my saying that leaving solitude is a gain, I say this because doing so makes us realize who we are and the degree of virtue we have. For people who are always recollected in solitude, however holy in their opinion they may be, don't know whether they are patient or humble, nor do they have any means of knowing this. How could it be known whether a man were valiant if he were not seen in battle? St. Peter thought he was very courageous; see how he acted when the occasion presented itself. But he came through that experience not trusting at all in himself, and as a result he trusted in God and subsequently suffered the martyrdom about which we know. (Ibid., 122-23)

For all of this emphasis on external service, however, Teresa does not leave prayer aside in the service of such tasks.

It's necessary to be on one's guard and careful in the performance of good works by having frequent interior recourse to God, even though these works are done in obedience and charity. And let souls believe me that it is not the length of time spent in prayer that benefits one; when the time is spent as well in good works, it is a great help in preparing the soul for the enkindling of love. The soul may thereby be better prepared in a very short time than through many hours of reflection. All must come from His hand. May He be blessed forever. (Ibid.)

OBEDIENCE IN OUR TIME

How shall we transfer Teresa's emphasis on obedience from her time to our own? Not only do most of us not live under the monastic rule of obedience to superiors, but we also are separated from the sixteenth century by five hundred years and the emergence of the democratic spirit. For twenty-first century people, influenced by the democratic traditions of political rebellion and the resurgence of democratic spirit through our new information technologies, obedience is a word fraught with danger. In a society that seeks to break off the shackles of abusive relationships of one group over another and destructive patterns of power, obedience is similarly a very treacherous topic. All too well, we know the power of the oppressor to use the terms of obedience to subjugate others.

But notice that Teresa is concerned with the cultivation of certain virtues that are necessary if we are to be servants of God, championing God's new causes in our time. We have just heard those virtues in her writings on obedience: solitude, patience, courage, humility. To begin to understand the magnificence of Teresa's thoughts on obedience, we must remember the starting point of her understanding of God: God is dwelling within each of us, already present, giving inspiration, inner wisdom, joy, and healing. This great One deigns to take us as companion in all arenas of earthly and heavenly life. From that starting point, it is only natural that Teresa should devise a way to suffer gladly with God, her spouse and lover, in deeds of service and new creation.

I suggest that a way to begin to look at our own callings in obedience is to examine the social arenas of our lives. Each of us lives and is sustained by a vast social fabric, ranging from our home as physical creatures of the earth to our sense of global citizenship; our citizenship within our local communities, state, and nation; our families, our churches, and our work environments. Everywhere our lives are under "social contract." In each realm, I find it very liberating to actually acknowledge a kind of creative tension that is inevitably present between what *I* want and need, what *others* want and need, and what we must learn to do *together* in order to accomplish our common goals. We do not live as people who have no limits on our desires. Can we instead learn to thrive as people who gladly suffer for others' good—or at least are willing to yield to the common purposes we share?

I have found it particularly useful to observe that all during my working life, I have chosen to put myself in extremely demanding communities—visionary communities, whose role has been to create some new form of community life in the world. I have discovered that I make myself obedient to the task that is required, which often has stretched me beyond my own imagined limits of endurance. And in honesty, I must admit that I have not yet learned the equanimity that Teresa espouses. Yet I have learned the virtues, discipline, and tenacity of service toward that which to me seems divinely inspired. In my book *Healing the Male Soul: Christianity and the Mythic Journey*, I have described these as the virtues of courage, fortitude, vision, and loving service (Judy, 1992).

Service, as the crucible for transformation, may come to us through the illness of a parent or spouse, in our commitment to our children, or to a great task that seems genuinely to come from God. Every day, in millions of lives around the world, dedication to task beyond personal gain is evidenced. We have somehow grown too silent in recent years about the necessity for such dedication, if our God is to actively shape our world through the action of our hands and hearts toward the vision of a human family, where love and respect draw forth each person's creative fire.

Thus, for our time, it is important to emphasize what Teresa called the practice of charity, as a discipline alongside the disciplines of meditative prayer and self-knowledge. In our previous discussion of the *Interior Castle*, you will recall that in Mansions III, through our own disciplined efforts, we spin the cocoon of transformation. Those disciplines are active modes of service within the family, community, church, and society, as well as the interior disciplines. Of course, as Teresa points out, there is a possibility of failing to heed the call to a deeper surrender, when both action and prayer come from our personal discipline. We have spoken at length about the surrender to God in prayer and the kind of transformation of the personality that can occur.

What kind of surrender is evident through our life of action that is parallel to the surrender in the interior that we learn in the prayers of quiet or union? I think that perhaps we learn to listen for a great summons, as Teresa heard herself summoned to found new houses of prayer. Thus, we may be prepared to hear a great task from God. Perhaps, like Teresa, this summons will not come until middle age. Or like Abraham, it may not come until old age. Do we not, deep within our hearts, hear some longing for love to express itself yet more fully through our relationships, our church, and our work in the world? If we are to "surrender into the arms of love" in our innermost prayer, we will find that God's love is dynamic. The divine arms of love will desire to reach out also through our actions, our values, and our life purpose, to create new arenas for love's presence in the church and the world. That is the nature of God. Such service to God is Teresa's highest form of obedience.

The greatness of Teresa's achievement may seem overwhelming. We may find ourselves looking at her accomplishments and imagine that we are not capable of such an achievement. Our task, of course, is not to imitate Teresa's accomplishment, but to find our own callings for service. Teresa was called to build a new kind of monastic community for women. Our tasks may be inspired by the everyday life of the workroom, the kitchen, the office, and the classroom. However, we also may be summoned by God to a challenge as great as Teresa's. "With God, nothing will prove impossible" (Luke 1:37 *footnote c*). Or as Teresa states, "Nothing is impossible when our Lord wants it" (Kavanaugh and Rodriguez, 1985, 102). To be open to such a summons is the spirit to which Teresa's life and work call us.

Her life shows a way to approach such a call: Work with every ally we can muster, be open to the struggle of political challenge, and test our vision with colleagues and foes alike. It will not necessarily be easy. Our first attempts may fail. Yet through such efforts, we may learn what is needed to sustain a new establishment of our vision in form.

Everywhere, I believe, God is now working such change and issuing such summons to service. If I have accurately described our time as a time of radical reorientation of the human spirit to the tasks of living as global citizens, then every institution stands in need of reform, from business to education, from the church to health care, from political structures to neighborhoods. We will undergo changes from the way we grow our food to the way we communicate. We can expect more dramatic changes for the duration of our lifetimes and for the foreseeable future. God is inviting each of us, in fact, to become futurists. How do you want to manifest a more loving world? Now is the time to listen for inner vision and to act. We have learned from our efforts at dealing with all problems on a national scale that such action from afar is not enough. The bad news of this discovery is that our cities and towns are currently fragmented.

The good news of this discovery is that every action—undertaken in love—no matter how small, is of absolute importance. There is a great liberty of spirit in the paradoxical nature of love-in-action. Every action, whether undertaken one-on-one or at the global level, contributes to God's reformation of the world. We can offer our arms as God's arms of love in our neighborhoods, families, towns, and cities. We can offer the divine arms of love a way to act through us by befriending the emerging aspirations of visionary people in parts of the world where rapid change is happening, such as Africa or the Balkans or Russia or Latin America or our inner cities. We may be inspired to contribute music or artistry to enliven this time of change. Whatever our contribution—in love—ennobles the human enterprise. From the simplest daily acts of kindness to the most complex social challenges, let us embrace God's arms of love embracing our world. Thus we will be outwardly conformed to God, as well as inwardly transformed. Teresa would invite no less from us.

"All must come from His hand. May He be blessed forever" (ibid., 123).

151

Exercises for Reflection and Prayer

1. Obedience to God

Central to Teresa's spirituality is the concept of obedience to God. In your prayer journal, write about your relationship to the concept of obedience to God. You may find it advantageous to think of other but related concepts, such as surrender to God or finding God's will for your life. How has your understanding of this concept changed through the years?

2. Spirituality of the Cross

Teresa speaks of her understanding of our relationship with God as manifesting through the image of the cross. She learned in her own life to "suffer gladly" for God in causes that she believed were inspired by God. When have you suffered for God? You may think of some quite graphic experience of pain in difficult situations, or you may think of a more gradual struggle for authenticity to a challenge that you perceived God was asking of you. Has Christ's suffering served to sustain you during these times? Do you relate more to Christ crucified, or to Christ as resurrected Lord? How do you relate in your own life to Teresa's dual theme of joy in God in prayer and suffering in God's service? Write on these themes in your journal.

3. What is God's calling to you?

Do you think of yourself as having a mission that God is asking you to do in the world? If your answer is yes, write about it and assess how your development of this mission is going. Ask God for further guidance at this time for its manifestation. If your immediate answer is no, then ask God for guidance about your life. The mission may be quite simple and not as involved in "creating new forms" as Teresa's mission. The danger in discussing other people's heroic service is that it tends to obscure our own call; we tend to think that our calling from God must be similar. It need not be. Be still and listen to God's desire for your life in respect to the many relationships our world offers.

4. Summing Up

Look back through all your writings and notes during the reading of this book or study of this material. Use a highlight marker and mark the 3 to 5 major themes you have been describing. You may find some interesting revelations by seeing what you have been most interested in writing about or what images have been most prominent in your prayers. Now ask yourself what areas of exploration seem most vital to you during the next few months of your spiritual journey.

APPENDIX

EXTERIOR WORLD

- -

INTERIOR WORLD

SURFACE LEVEL AWARENESS:

Sensory awareness / Discursive thinking / Ordinary mental process

- -

SYMBOLIC LEVEL AWARENESS:

Imagination/Imagery as tool to deeper quiet/Emotional awareness

- -

ULTIMATE AWARENESS:

God "enthroned on the heart"/Divine "arms of love"
Experiences of being taught by God in deep silence

eresa's descriptions of our deepening self-understanding and awareness of God, as we explore the Mansions of our souls, corresponds well to this understanding of a movement from surface level awareness, through symbolic level awareness to ultimate awareness. When we place the description of the seven Mansions alongside this diagram, we discover that the Mansions describe experiences related to these different qualities of our souls. That process of emerging experience can be diagrammed as follows:

EXTERIOR WORLD

Mansions I   -

INTERIOR WORLD

SURFACE LEVEL AWARENESS:

Mansions II   *Sensory awareness / Discursive thinking /*
                Ordinary mental process

Mansions III   -

Mansions IV   SYMBOLIC LEVEL AWARENESS:

Mansions V   *Imagination/Imagery as tool to deeper quiet/*
                Emotional awareness

Mansions VI   -

ULTIMATE AWARENESS:

God "enthroned on the heart"/Divine "arms of love"
Experiences of being taught by God in deep silence

155

In Mansions I, we are very much immersed in the exterior world. It is our home, there is very little self-awareness or understanding of our spiritual depths. In Mansions II, we begin our journey through our surface level awareness. We take in information about the possibility of a deeper spiritual life, but are very much dependent upon exterior sources for the cultivation of this interior life. In Mansions III, we utilize our ordinary mental processes and discursive thinking by engaging in disciplined practices of prayer, reflection on scripture and other forms of the prayer of recollection. During these meditative prayer experiences, however, we may glimpse a new kind of spiritual imagination emerging, in which an interior living Christ may manifest or in which memories are accessed and healing is given before the presence of God. Those kinds of experiences emerge from what I am calling the symbolic level of awareness. Thus, Mansions III becomes the bridge from surface level awareness to the symbolic level of awareness.

In Mansions IV, V, and VI, Teresa describes a great variety of experiences associated with the symbolic level awareness. Many of these are very intense in their emotionality. This is her "native" realm in terms of the interior visions that are so frequently a part of her prayer life. Even so, through the touches of the prayer of quiet and then the extended prayer of union, the level of ultimate awareness with its silent perception of the embrace of God, begins to manifest and to quiet even her interior imagination. Thus, Mansions VI is a bridge toward this deeper quiet.

Finally, Teresa's interior certainty of union with God takes such deep root within her that a sense of divine presence pervades her daily life and her decision process. She comes to feel God-with-her in the midst of every moment. Her will and the divine will are joined together. Then, she lives in the exterior world from a deep interior sense of divine presence.

BIBLIOGRAPHY/
SOURCES

Arrien, Angeles, 1993. *The Four-Fold Way: Walking the Paths of the Warrior, Teacher, Healer, and Visionary.* San Francisco: HarperSanFrancisco.

Auclair, M., 1988. *St. Teresa of Avila.* Petersham, Mass.: St. Bede's Publications. (Reprint of 1953 Pantheon Edition, trans. Kathleen Pond.)

Bilinkoff, J., 1989. *The Avila of St. Teresa.* Ithaca, N.Y.: Cornell University Press.

Bragdon, E., 1990. *The Call of Spiritual Emergency.* San Francisco: Harper & Row.

Chorpenning, J. F., O.S.F.S., 1992. *The Divine Romance: Teresa of Avila's Narrative Theology.* Chicago: Loyola University Press.

A Course in Miracles, 1975. Huntington Station, N.Y.: Foundation for Inner Peace.

du Boulay, S., 1991. *Teresa of Avila.* London: Hodder & Stoughton.

Elliott, J., 1963. *Imperial Spain, 1469–1716.* New York: Saint Martin's Press.

Flinders, C. L., 1993. *Enduring Grace: Living Portraits of Seven Women Mystics.* San Francisco: HarperSanFrancisco.

Fox, M., 1983. *Original Blessing: A Primer in Creation Spirituality.* Santa Fe: Bear & Co.

Green, D., 1989. *Gold in the Crucible: Teresa of Avila and the Western Mystical Tradition.* Shaftesbury, Dorset, Great Britain: Longmead.

Greenwell, B., 1990. *Energies of Transformation: A Guide to the Kundalini Process.* Campbell, Calif.: Shakti River Press.

Grof, S. and C., ed. 1989. *Spiritual Emergency: When Personal Transformation Becomes a Crisis.* Los Angeles: J. P. Tarcher, Inc.

Grof, S. and C., 1990. *The Stormy Search for the Self: A Guide to Personal Growth Through Transformational Crisis.* Los Angeles: J. P. Tarcher.

Hamilton, E., 1985. *The Life of Saint Teresa of Avila.* Westminster, Md.: Christian Classics.

Judy, D., 1991. *Christian Meditation and Inner Healing.* New York: Crossroad.

_____, 1992. *Healing the Male Soul: Christianity and the Mythic Journey.* New York: Crossroad.

Kavanaugh, K., and O. Rodriguez, trans., 1974. *The Collected Works of St. John of the Cross.* Washington, D.C.: ICS Publications.

_____, trans., 1976. *The Collected Works of St. Teresa of Avila, Vol. 1.* Washington, D.C.: ICS Publications.

_____, trans., 1980. *The Collected Works of St. Teresa of Avila, Vol. 2.* Washington, D.C.: ICS Publications.

_____, trans., 1985. *The Collected Works of St. Teresa of Avila, Vol. 3.* Washington, D.C.: ICS Publications.

Keating, T., 1992. *Invitation to Love: The Way of Christian Contemplation.* Rockport, Mass., and Shaftesbury, Dorset, U.K.: Element.

Kierkegaard, S., 1958. *Edifying Discourses, A Selection,* ed. P. L. Holmer, trans. D. F. and L. M. Swenson. New York: Harper & Row.

Lincoln, V., 1984. *Teresa: A Woman. A Biography of Teresa of Avila.* Albany, N.Y.: University of New York Press.

Luti, J. M., 1991. *Teresa of Avila's Way.* Collegeville: Minn.: The Liturgical Press.

Morello, S. A., 1995. *Lectio Divina and the Practice of Teresian Prayer.* Washington D.C.: ICS Publications.

Mottola, A., trans., 1964. *The Spiritual Exercises of St. Ignatius.* Garden City, N.Y.: Doubleday-Image.

Polster, M. F., 1992. *Eve's Daughters: The Forbidden Heroism of Women.* San Francisco: Jossey-Bass.

Romano, C. 1981. "A Psycho-Spiritual History of Teresa of Avila: A Woman's Perspective" in *Western Spirituality: Historical Roots, Ecumenical Routes,* ed. M. Fox. Santa Fe: Bear & Co., 261-95.

Singer, J., 1990. *Seeing Through the Visible World: Jung, Gnosis, and Chaos.* New York: Harper & Row.

Sugden, E., ed., 1921, 1968. *The Standard Sermons of John Wesley, Vol 1.* London: Epworth Press.

Underhill, E., 1961. *Mysticism: A Study in the Nature and Development of Man's Spiritual Consciousness.* New York: E. P. Dutton.

Wakefield, G., ed., 1983. *The Westminster Dictionary of Christian Spirituality.* Philadelphia: Westminster Press.